# UNDARKENED SKIES

# UNDARKENED SKIES

## THE AMERICAN AIRCRAFT BUILDING PROGRAMME OF THE FIRST WORLD WAR

PAUL R. HARE

FONTHILL

Fonthill Media Language Policy

Fonthill Media publishes in the international English language market. One language edition is published worldwide. As there are minor differences in spelling and presentation, especially with regard to American English and British English, a policy is necessary to define which form of English to use. The Fonthill Policy is to use the form of English native to the author. Paul R. Hare was born and educated in London; therefore British English has been adopted in this publication.

Fonthill Media Limited
Fonthill Media LLC
www.fonthillmedia.com
office@fonthillmedia.com

First published in the United Kingdom and the United States of America 2017

British Library Cataloguing in Publication Data:
A catalogue record for this book is available from the British Library



ISBN 978-1-78155-651-1



Typeset in 10.5pt on 13pt Sabon
Printed and bound in England

# Acknowledgments

In the three decades of research that culminated in this book, the author has received help, with information or with photographs, from many individuals and organisations to whom his gratitude is owed, and whose contribution to its completion is hereby gratefully acknowledged. These include: Aircraft Engine Historical Society; Gregory Alegi; the late J. M. Bruce; Robert Casari; Nick Forder; Colin Huston; Kevin Kelly; Walter Kudlick; Lannie & Joe Liggera; Massachusetts Institute of Technology; Leo Opdycke; Rolls-Royce Heritage Trust; United States Air Force Museum; and numerous individual members of Cross and Cockade International.

A special and most heartfelt 'thank you' is long overdue to my wife, Linda, for her patience and support throughout the lengthy process of the preparation of this book, and also to thank my good friend Bob Bellisio, a retired teacher, who proofread key passages of the manuscript, and whose suggestions were always helpful, although any mistakes, of course, remain my own responsibility.

# CONTENTS


*Acknowledgements* 5
*Author's Note* 9
*Introduction* 11
1 Aviation in America before the War 13
2 America Enters the War 23
3 The US Standardised Aero Engine 31
4 Preliminary Proposals 37
5 The Mission to Europe 43
6 Financing the Plan 59
7 The Orders are Placed 62
8 Curtiss JN-4 73
9 Standard J-1 75
10 Bristol Scout D 77
11 Royal Aircraft Factory S.E.5a 80
12 SPAD S.VII and S.XIII 84
13 Curtiss R-4 and R-6 87
14 Bristol F.2B Fighter 89
15 Caproni Bombers 95
16 Handley Page O/400 98
17 Martin MB-1 103
18 De Havilland DH.4 105
19 USD-9 111
20 LUSAC-11 114
21 Growing Dissatisfaction 119
22 The Air Service 'Over There' 127
23 The Situation at the End of the War 132
*Conclusion* 138
*Appendix I: The Liberty Engine* 145
*Appendix II: DH.4 Statistics* 152
*Appendix III: Aircraft Production Facts* 154
*Bibliography* 155
*Index* 158

# Author's Note

Although this book is largely concerned with activities in America, and much of the research necessary to its preparation was conducted in that country, the author of this work is English, and therefore the narrative employs British English spelling and grammar, except in any direct quotations from contemporary documents where the spelling and style of the original have been maintained.

Similarly, the machine designed by Geoffrey de Havilland as a day bomber when built in England to the original design is referred to as a 'D.H.4', while the modified version, built in America, is designated, as it was in that country, as a 'DH-4'.

# Introduction

Soon after entering the war, in April 1917, American propaganda promised that she would 'darken the skies over Europe' by sending over 'the Greatest Aerial Armada ever seen'.

Encouraged by the French Government, the America Government promised to build no less than 22,000 aeroplanes within a year and to field, and to maintain, a force of 4,000 machines, all of the latest type, over the Western Front during 1918. This was to provide adequate air support for her own ground troops, but was also seen as a way to use her huge industrial strength to bypass the squalor of the war in the trenches, and so bring an end to the stalemate of attrition into which the war had descended.

In May 1917, Howard Coffin, Head of the Aircraft Production Board, confidently predicted that 3,500 American-built aeroplanes would be in the air by the end of the year, and that up to 100,000 could be produced within two years. The programme started off well enough, with the US Government quickly providing the sum of $640 million, the largest single allocation ever made up to that date, to fund it, and adding even more funds whenever they were asked for. A group of engineers and production experts, both from the military and from industry, was sent to visit England, France, and Italy in order to select the most up-to-date combat aeroplanes available, to negotiate production licences, obtain drawings, and arrange for sample machines to be shipped back to the United States, all of which they achieved in just a few weeks.

The aeroplane was an American invention, and America was the home of Henry Ford and of mass production, with a manufacturing capacity equal to or even greater than that of all of the countries of Europe combined. America had 'a tradition of doing things on a grand scale', yet, by the time of the Armistice on 11 November 1918, just 196 American-built aeroplanes were in active service in France—a number unable, even in the unlikely event of their all being airborne at once, to darken much of the sky.

In addition, the whole programme was already the subject of several official investigations before the war was even over, and has since been widely condemned as a failure, even by some of those involved in it. Criticisms can be made throughout; in the selection of the designs to be mass-produced, in the way in which the programme was managed, and in the reliance placed upon companies that had never previously built aeroplanes. Technical difficulties, unforeseen at the outset, certainly slowed production, as did the substitution of the Liberty engine in almost every design adopted. Mismanagement, malfeasance, corruption, and pure greed have all been cited as causes of the programme's failure, and some evidence can be found to support all these claims, as it probably could be in any government-funded programme, especially one of this magnitude. Yet was corruption the root of the problem, or was the whole plan simply over-ambitious, and so incapable of being achieved within the timescale set?

Let us carefully examine all the facts, starting, of course, at the very beginning.

DH-4s of the 135th Aero Squadron in France in 1918. Much publicity was made of such units to show that America was taking an active part in the war, even though her contribution to the aerial effort fell a long way short of her promises and predictions.

# 1

# Aviation in America before the War

It is generally, if not universally, accepted that the aeroplane was invented in America, with the Wright Brothers spending four years developing their control system by kite flying and gliding experiments, before making the first powered flights at Kitty Hawk on the North Carolina coast, on the morning of 17 December 1903. They spent the next two years improving their design, developing it into the world's first practical aeroplane, and then stopped flying altogether while they attempted to market their invention, fearful that public demonstrations would allow others to copy their design. Tentative approaches had already been made to both the British and American Governments, as the Wrights then thought only of selling in terms of military contracts, not private sales. However, at that time, they believed that the aeroplane would make future wars practically impossible since the facilities for the reconnaissance it provided would make new military installations and troop movements easy to observe and so remove any possibility of a surprise attack.

Meanwhile, both in Europe and America, other inventors were hard at work, striving independently to solve the mystery of flight. The Brazilian Alberto Santos-Dumont made the first aeroplane flights in Europe during 1906, and on 12 November, he covered a distance of 721 feet in twenty-one seconds; others, most notably Henri Farman, soon followed his example making a circular flight, the first in Europe, on 19 January 1908. Progress thereafter was fairly rapid, with flights steadily becoming longer, flying becoming faster and higher, and aircraft with increased reliability.

Back in America, Glenn H. Curtiss, piloting a machine built by the Aerial Experimental Association, whose members included Alexandra Graham Bell, won a prize offered by the magazine *Scientific American* for the first preannounced public flight in America; on 4 July 1908, he flew

The 1905 Wright *Flyer*, the world's first practical powered aeroplane possessing effective control in all three axes. It would be years before any other design could rival its control.

5,080 feet at Hammondsport in upper New York State, staying aloft for one minute and forty-two seconds.

In England, the ex-patriot American cowboy, showman, and kite enthusiast Samuel Franklin Cody made that country's first powered flight in a machine built at government expense. On 16 October 1908, he flew 1,390 feet across Farnborough Common in the aptly named *British Army Aeroplane No.1*; unfortunately, he crash-landed as he attempted to turn to avoid a clump of trees. However, soon after this momentous event, the British Government decided that the expense of its aeronautical experiments had been too great considering the results obtained and decided that, at least for the time being, it would leave the development of the aeroplane to private industry, and then simply buy whatever aeroplanes it needed. In reality, it would be several years before the aeroplane was sufficiently developed so that any such purchases could be made.

Having spent $50,000 funding Professor Samuel P. Langley's attempts to achieve powered flight contemporaneously with the Wrights' own experiments, only to see each take-off attempt fail, the US Government also chose to leave aircraft development in private hands. However, this did not satisfy Cortland Bishop, President of the American Aero Club, who frequently sent papers regarding progress in aviation to President Theodore Roosevelt, urging him to take action. Roosevelt, in turn, instructed the Army to seriously investigate the possibility of employing aircraft for military purposes. As a result, the Wrights' next efforts at lobbying were finally rewarded; on 23 December 1907, specification No. 486 was issued, giving details of the requirements for a flying machine for military use. Carefully written around the known performance of the Wright *Flyer*, this document called for a machine that could carry two people, fly at 40 mph, and stay aloft for at least an hour. It was required to 'be capable of dismounting and loading onto an army wagon for transporting' and to 'permit an intelligent man to become proficient in its use within a reasonable length of time'. A range of 125 miles was also stipulated.

Originally, the Wright Brothers had asked $100,000 each for their *Flyers*, believing that no rival could match their mastery of the air, but they had now reduced the price to $25,000, a sum that was still beyond what could normally be spent without congressional approval. However, the Army avoided this need by reallocating some funds left over from a provision for the Spanish–American War, which had lain dormant since the ending of that conflict almost a decade before.

It was expected that the Wright Brothers would be the only ones to bid against the specification, but by the time the deadline came, a total of forty-one bids had been received at prices ranging from $1,000 to $1 million. Many would-be bidders were unable to put up the bond of 10 per cent of the asking price required to bid, and some bids were immediately rejected as frivolous, along with one that ambitiously offered a speed of 500 mph; finally, a shortlist of three 'possibles' emerged. Of these, the lowest bid was from a Mr F. J. Scott of Chicago, who had set his price at $1,000 simply because $100 was the most he could offer as a bond, but on further consideration, his bid was then withdrawn. This left the Wrights and a $20,000 bid from Augustus Moore Herring, an experimenter who had assisted Octave Chanute with his gliding trials and had visited the Wrights in their camp at Kitty Hawk; he also later briefly became associated with Glenn Curtiss. Herring, however, turned out to be unable to fulfil his offer to supply the Army with a flying machine, and so, almost by default, on 10 February, the Wright Brothers, who had therefore submitted the only viable bid, received Signal Corps order No. 3619, the first ever placed for an aeroplane.

Since lighter-than-air craft were then still being considered as a possible alternative to aeroplanes, an order for a dirigible balloon was placed with the showman balloonist Thomas Scott Baldwin at the same time at

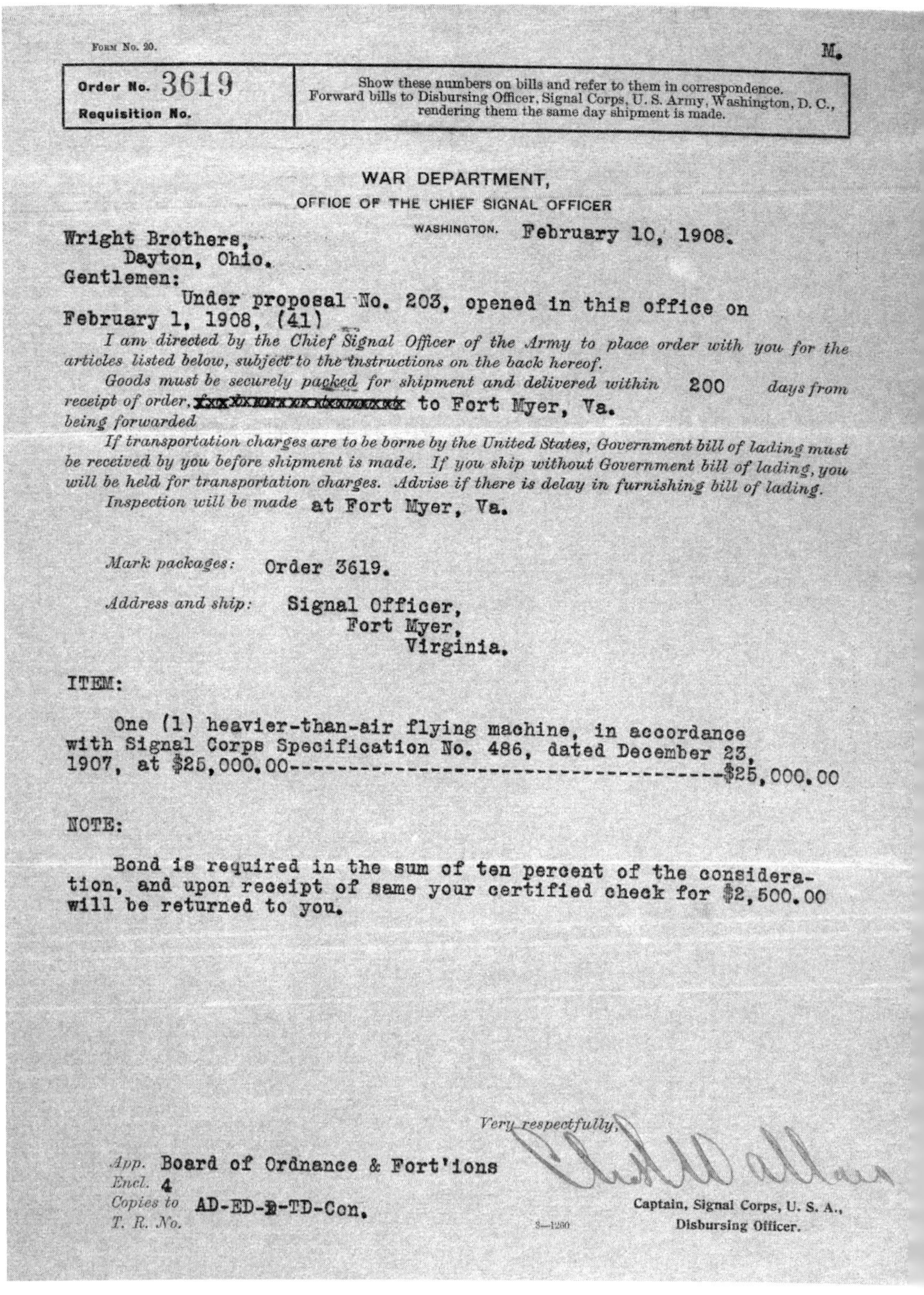

FORM No. 20. M.

| Order No. 3619<br>Requisition No. | Show these numbers on bills and refer to them in correspondence.<br>Forward bills to Disbursing Officer, Signal Corps, U. S. Army, Washington, D. C.,<br>rendering them the same day shipment is made. |
|---|---|

WAR DEPARTMENT,
OFFICE OF THE CHIEF SIGNAL OFFICER
WASHINGTON. February 10, 1908.

Wright Brothers,
Dayton, Ohio.
Gentlemen:

Under proposal No. 203, opened in this office on February 1, 1908, (41)

*I am directed by the Chief Signal Officer of the Army to place order with you for the articles listed below, subject to the instructions on the back hereof.*

*Goods must be securely packed for shipment and delivered within* 200 *days from receipt of order,* xxxxxxxxxxxxxxxxxxx to Fort Myer, Va. *being forwarded*

*If transportation charges are to be borne by the United States, Government bill of lading must be received by you before shipment is made. If you ship without Government bill of lading, you will be held for transportation charges. Advise if there is delay in furnishing bill of lading.*

*Inspection will be made* at Fort Myer, Va.

*Mark packages:* Order 3619.

*Address and ship:* Signal Officer,
Fort Myer,
Virginia.

ITEM:

One (1) heavier-than-air flying machine, in accordance with Signal Corps Specification No. 486, dated December 23, 1907, at $25,000.00------------------------------------$25,000.00

NOTE:

Bond is required in the sum of ten percent of the consideration, and upon receipt of same your certified check for $2,500.00 will be returned to you.

*Very respectfully,*

*App.* Board of Ordnance & Fort'ions
*Encl.* 4
*Copies to* AD-ED-B-TD-Con.
*T. R. No.*

8—1260

Captain, Signal Corps, U. S. A.,
Disbursing Officer.

The official order given to the Wright Brothers to supply the US Army with its first aeroplane, setting out the terms and conditions under which it was to be supplied.

a cost of $6,750. This was powered by an engine built by Glenn Curtiss and was delivered in July 1908, three operators then being trained in its use; however, it failed to realise its anticipated potential and the Army's attention became focused on heavier-than-air flight.

Military aviation in America had begun, as it had in many other countries, with balloons. During the Civil War (1861–65), balloon observers had relayed their observation to troops on the ground by telegraph, hence the involvement of the Signal Corps in their operation. The Army aviation units would remain under their umbrella, although with various differing titles, until 1918.

With Wilbur Wright away in France, demonstrating the *Flyer* to potential purchasers in Europe, it fell to Orville to carry out the trials for the US Army. The machine was delivered on 1 September to Fort Myer, Virginia, close to the nation's capital, with flying beginning a few days later, after the machine had been assembled.

At first, all went well, with Orville setting several new records for endurance, but on 17 September, a split developed in one propeller blade, causing it to distort and thereby creating an out-of-balance force that further damaged the machine. It then crashed to the ground from a

The Wright *Flyer* arrives at Fort Myer, Virginia, in September 1908 on a trailer towed behind a 1907 Lozier touring car, ready to begin its acceptance trials. Soon, aeroplanes would replace observation balloons throughout the world's air forces.

height of around 100 feet. The *Flyer* was a total wreck, Orville suffered numerous injuries—the most serious of which was a badly broken leg—and his passenger, Lt Thomas Selfridge, who had been a member of the Aerial Experimental Association, as well as being trained as a dirigible pilot, was killed.

It was not until the following June that the Wrights were able to deliver a replacement *Flyer* to Fort Myer to complete the trials. This *Flyer* was of a slightly modified design, but powered by the engine recovered from the wreck of its predecessor. This time, Wilbur, now returned from Europe, accompanied his brother. The tests proceeded without any further hitches, and the machine was formally accepted by the US Army on 2 August 1909. As the Signal Corps' first aeroplane, it was given the serial number SC1 and the Wrights were paid $30,000—a sum that included a bonus of $5,000 for having exceeded the stipulated minimum speed by 5 mph.

By 7 October, SC1 had been transferred to a new training ground at College Park, Maryland, where Wilbur fulfilled the brothers' final obligation under their contract by giving instruction to Lt Frank P. Lahm and 2Lt Fredric E. Humphreys, both of whom flew solo on 26 October. However, on 5 November, both were aboard SC1, with Lahm at the controls, when the machine crashed while turning at a low altitude. Fortunately, neither was injured and the Wrights carried out the necessary repairs free of charge as a good will gesture. Both Lahm and Humphreys returned to other duties soon after, but not before Humphreys had completed giving instruction to Benjamin D. Foulois, who had previously piloted the dirigible, until it became increasing leaky and was sold off at auction. Foulois then remained the Signal Corps' only active pilot until 1911.

SC1 made its last flight, piloted by Foulois, on 8 February 1911 and was presented to the Smithsonian Institute later that year. On 13 March, the Army ordered two replacement aeroplanes, another Wright and a Curtiss—both pushers. However, delivery was far from immediate, and so, when the Army wished to put on show of force in Texas, presumably to discourage Mexican revolutionaries from venturing across the Rio Grande, Foulois was obliged borrow a Wright *Flyer* privately owned by the publisher of Collier's magazine in order to undertake the required aerial reconnaissance.

When the two new machines, SC2 and SC3, were finally delivered, the Signal Corps were able to field three machines simultaneously, proudly photographing them in the air together.

Major George Owen Squier, who had been Orville's first passenger at Fort Myer, took over command of the Aeronautical Division in April 1911 and began to train new pilots at Fort Sam Houston in Texas. He was soon

The US Army's entire 1911 aerial fleet, SC2, SC3, and a Wright *Flyer*, which was on loan from a private owner, all airborne together. Already, America was falling far behind other nations in the development of military aeronautics.

moved on to a new posting, becoming military *attaché* to the US Embassy in London in 1912.

A total of eight aeroplanes were delivered to the Signal Corps during 1911, followed by eleven in 1912, seven in 1913, and twelve in 1914. Yet obsolescence and crashes took their toll, and on 18 July 1914, when the Aviation Section was established by Public Law 63-143, it possessed considerably fewer than twenty serviceable aeroplanes and had a total manpower of just nineteen officers and 101 other ranks.

Outside the USA, military aviation initially progressed at a similar pace. However, under the more obvious threat of war, European aviation accelerated more rapidly, soon leaving America far behind.

France's *Aéronautique Militaire* was created as a separate branch of the army in October 1910, although it was not until March 1912 that a law was passed to formalise its existence. Pilots were training in the newly established civilian training schools, the first military pilots' certificates being awarded during 1911. By the summer of 1912, five *Escadrilles* (squadrons) had been established, this number growing to twenty-one by 1914, with a total of 132 operational aeroplanes between them.

Germany initially put its faith in the Zeppelin airships, but bought its first military aeroplane in 1910. Progress with heavier-than-air flight was slow at first, but Germany then began a programme of rapid expansion in an effort to match its air service to that of France.

Britain, having been awoken to the threat to its security as demonstrated by Louis Bleriot's flight across the Channel in July 1909, first expanded its 'Military Ballooning' operations to embrace aeroplanes and then, in 1911, established the Air Battalion of the Royal Engineers to take over all aerial activity. This unit was absorbed into the newly established Royal Flying

Corps the following spring, and a competition announced, open to all, and with large cash prizes to be held in the summer of 1912. This was to select the aeroplanes with which the new RFC should be equipped. Meanwhile, in order to encourage the growth of the inchoate aeroplane industry, small orders were placed with a variety of companies. Officers seeking to join had first to obtain an Aero Club pilot's licence at their own expense, but were given a grant of £75 towards the cost on their acceptance as military pilots.

America remained distant, politically as well as geographically, from Europe, and, lacking the stimulus of a pending war, its air services remained small and rather underfunded, being just fourteenth in the world's ranking in terms of expenditure on military aviation. In the period between 1908 and 1913, Germany spent the equivalent of over £5 million on military aviation and France over £4 million, while, in the same period, America spent just under £90,000, less even than Brazil. In 1915, with the rest of the world expanding its aerial arms, America's Aviation Section received just the dollar equivalent of £50,000 with which to fund its entire operation.

America's neutrality added to its isolation from developments in Europe as none of the combatant nations, in which almost all of the technical advances in aviation were currently being made, were keen to share information with a neutral country that could, legitimately, share it with their enemy. In March 1915, the Federal Government established the National Advisory Committee for Aeronautics (NACA) stating that 'it shall be the duty of the advisory committee for aeronautics to supervise and direct the scientific study of the problems of flight with a view to their practical solution'. However, their study was directed purely at the problems of mechanical flight, not those of combat.

The Wrights sold just fourteen aeroplanes to the US Government, all of them pushers, a design layout from which the company never really advanced and, following the death of Wilbur in 1912, Orville lost much of his interest in flying and so the Wright Company fell into a decline. Of course, other American aeroplane makers came into existence, most notably the Wrights' arch rival Curtiss, who started aircraft and engine manufacture at Hammondsport, and the Glenn L. Martin Company, which was founded in 1912 and soon began to sell its products, one by one, to the US Army. During 1915, Glenn L. Martin merged with the remains of the Wright Company to form Wright-Martin.

The Curtiss Aeroplane and Motor Company met with the greater success, selling its JN series machines in small numbers to the Signal Corps and then receiving much larger orders from Britain, where the type was adopted for training. This necessitated a move from sleepy Hammondsport to much larger premises in Buffalo. Its flying boats were also purchased both by Britain and by the US Navy.

Thus, by 1916, the output of American aircraft factories had increased, with some, especially Curtiss, producing dozens of machines, most of them for export to Europe. At the same time, European factories had already expanded to build aeroplanes by the thousand.

The Aviation Section of the Signal Corps expanded slowly, continuing to support the troops based in Texas to counter the threat of a possible war with revolutionary Mexico. They established bases at San Diego and at Manila, in the Philippines, but by the beginning of 1916, they possessed only twenty-three active aeroplanes, thirty-six having been damaged, destroyed, or simply written-off as out of date since 1909.

The year 1916 saw the eight Curtiss JN-3s from Fort Sam Houston move south, travelling by rail into Mexico, as part of a punitive expedition in retaliation for the revolutionary leader Pancho Villa's raid on Columbus, New Mexico. However, they proved underpowered and unable to cope with the climatic conditions, and although some useful reconnaissance flight were made, within a month, only two aircraft remained serviceable and more powerful replacements had to be obtained, again from Curtiss.

The Mexican campaign had clearly demonstrated the inadequacies of America's air service, and aware of the possibility that America would eventually enter the far more challenging war in Europe, on 3 June 1916, Congress adopted the National Defense Act. Part of this act authorised

Lt Chapman about to take-off in a Signal Corps Curtiss for a reconnaissance mission in Mexico during 1916.

the increase of the Aviation Section to eight squadrons, with a total of 148 officers, and as many enlisted men as the President chose to allow. On 29 August, Congress approved a total budget of $13 million for military aviation, to be shared between the Signal Corps and the National Guard.

The Council of National Defense was created towards the end of 1916 to regulate contact between the Army and industry, which hitherto had been conducted on a rather informal basis. Chaired by the Secretary of War Newton D. Baker, its members included the Secretaries of the Navy, Labor, and the Interior, together with a number of prominent businessmen. Its role was to plan how industry could best use its resources to aid mobilisation in time of war, but it acted without haste, wrongly assuming that war was still many years in the future.

Up to January 1917, a grand total of 118 service aeroplanes had been delivered to the US Army, sixty-four of them manufactured during 1916, with purchases during early 1917 following a similar pattern. However, wastage, due to a number of causes including crashes, continually eroded the number available for use; at the beginning of April, the Aviation Section of the Signal Corps possessed just fifty-five serviceable aeroplanes for field operations, fifty-one of which were already obsolete, together with a similar number of training machines. Its personnel strength included just 126 officers, not all of them qualified pilots, and a little over 1,000 other ranks.

The situation in industry was little better, although there was a growing number of companies who listed their business as Aeroplane Manufacture. Of these, only five—Curtiss, L.W.F, Standard, Thomas-Morse, and Wright-Martin—had ever completed more than ten machines each. During 1916, both Curtiss and Wright-Martin had been bought up by Wall Street Investment Syndicates—Curtiss because of its ongoing contracts to supply aeroplanes to Great Britain and Wright-Martin largely because, as successors to the Wright Brothers company, they held the key patent on lateral control and so could claim a royalty on every aeroplane built.

Aero engine manufacture was largely limited to Curtiss, whose 90-hp water-cooled V8 OX-5 engine powered the JN series of aeroplanes, and Hall-Scott of Berkeley, California, builders of engines for rail cars as well as aeroplanes, whose engines had a power to weight ratio remarkable for the time, due both to their very efficient design and an extensive use of aluminium. The General Vehicle Company of Long Island, New York, built a small number of Le Rhône rotary engines under licence, and Wright-Martin were beginning production of the 150-hp direct drive variant of the Hispano-Suiza V8 in response to an order from the French Government. This engine was also being further developed and extensively manufactured in Europe, but America production, of all types, was limited both by manufacturing capacity and by demand.

2

# America Enters the War

On 4 April 1917, the US Senate—in response to an appeal from President Woodrow Wilson for the USA to declare war on Germany—voted eighty-two to six in favour, a decision endorsed two days later by the House of Representatives by a vote of 373 to fifty. On that same day, 6 April 1917, the USA formally entered the war.

Although in February 1917, after Germany had resumed its policy of unrestricted submarine warfare and had begun torpedoing American merchant ships without warning, Congress had voted to increase spending on armaments—little progress had been made in doing so before the declaration of war. The US Army was small, especially for a nation of her size, and recruitment, largely by conscription, began immediately after her entry into the war. However, it was in its industrial strength that America saw its best contribution to the war, rather than in simply committing its reserves of manpower to the slaughter of the trenches.

Her manufacturing capacity already compared favourably with that of the whole of Europe, with mass production methods, then known as 'the American System of Manufacture', both increasing output and reducing cost. Although now often associated with Henry Ford, this system—in which machinery, jigs, and processes operated by unskilled workers, largely replacing skilled craftsmen, to produce identical interchangeable parts—had been employed in the fabrication of blocks for rigging ships, and in producing guns, sewing machines, and farm implements long before it was applied to the manufacture of the motor cars, for which it became best known.

America liked to embrace modernity and saw in the aeroplane, which had been invented in America, a way to defeat the enemy quickly and more cleanly than by continuing the apparent stalemate of trench warfare. Although less than two decades old, the aeroplane was already a key element in the conduct of the war, its many tactical roles including reconnaissance, aerial photography, artillery observation, and bombing, all under the protection of fighters, which also attempted to prevent the enemy's aeroplanes from carrying out similar roles. Strategic bombing, the destruction of facilities outside the combat zone in order to reduce the enemy's capacity to wage war, was of increasing significance in the Allies' war plans and would be seen as a way of utilising America's resources to win the war quickly and cleanly, doing things the American way. So America quickly decided that building a large fleet of aeroplanes was an essential part of her plans to help win the war. The problem was that her officials had no idea of which aeroplanes she should build, or exactly who should build them.

Col. George O. Squier, while military *attaché* in London, visited the British RFC in France in December 1914 in order to acquaint himself with the conduct of the war, and the flying services contribution to it, but it was already a very different war. In 1916, he had returned to the USA to resume command of the Aviation Section, before becoming Chief Signal Officer in February 1917. Almost immediately after the declaration of war, he suggested that aeronautical experts from America's allies—England, France, and Italy—be invited to come over to the USA to give advice regarding the expansion of the air service to equip to take part in modern war. The British and French promptly complied, each sending both flying officers and suitably qualified civilians to assist their new allies in any way possible, augmenting the trade mission that had been in place since 1914 largely to secure supplies of war materials for their own countries.

The new British mission was considered sufficiently important to be led by Foreign Secretary Arthur Balfour himself, and it included L. W. B. Rees VC, RFC, who was then convalescing after suffering a wound in his thigh during the action for which he had been awarded Britain's highest gallantry award, and who had been promoted to temporary Lieutenant Colonel for the duty. The party travelled first by train to Scotland, then sailed from Greenock to Halifax, Nova Scotia, and, again by train, to Washington DC, arriving on 22 April 1917. While in America, they did all that they could, both to promote co-operation between the two nations and to assist wherever possible with own America's war efforts. The newspaper magnate Lord Northcliffe also went, largely to promote British interests, staying several months, and visiting a considerable number of factories while in America.

The Balfour mission left for England on 23 May, but the US Army was so taken with Rees—for his modesty and obvious bravery—that Major Squier formally requested he be allowed to remain to assist in the development of

The Allied Aviation Mission to the US. Lt-Col. L. W. B. Rees VC is in the centre and Lord Northcliffe is second from the right in a rather ill-fitting bowler hat. Although Arthur Balfour was the leader of the mission, in American eyes, it was Rees who was its star, as his position in the line-up confirms.

the air services. This request was granted and he stayed in America for the rest of the year, touring the country and lecturing on Military Aviation at training camps and military academies, finally returning home aboard the RMS *Carmania*, which was then serving as a troop ship, in January 1918.

Less than three weeks after America's entry into the war, on 26 April, during a Parliamentary debate on Britain's air services, the independent MP for East Hertfordshire, Noel Pemberton Billing, commented:

> It would be a very useful thing for the Allies if America could put from 3,000 to 5,000 bomb dropping aeroplanes on the Western Front. It would be quite possible for the American nation, without any great strain on their resources of either personnel or material to build 5,000 or 10,000 aeroplanes in the next six to eight months.

He considered that it would be wrong for the Americans to have to repeat the mistakes Britain had made over the past two and a half years and questioned, rhetorically, what commercial cause had so far prevented the necessary drawings and specifications from being sent. Italy made an alternative proposal, suggesting that demonstration aircraft be sent, at the expense of the Italian Government, with a view to promoting sales to the USA. This suggestion was not accepted. Instead, a mission, headed by Major R. Perfetti, who had previously been to America to buy war materials on behalf of the Italians, finally arrived in New York on 27 June.

Meanwhile, Captains Benjamin Foulois and Edgar Gorrell began preparing a proposal for the expansion of the Aeronautical Division. This was aimed at meeting the air support needs of the fairly modest army that was all it was initially thought America would be able to field in the near future. Working on the basis of one aeroplane for every thousand troops, and allowing for wastage, they calculated that 2,500 aeroplanes would be required, a number that the existing industry might, with reasonable confidence, be expected to build, and the flying services to expand enough to operate. Congress therefore approved an appropriation of $10.8 million on 21 May 1917, followed by a further $43.4 million two weeks later, with which to fund that level of expansion.

However, the situation regarding which aeroplanes to choose remained extremely uncertain. Secretary of War Newton D. Baker commented: 'There was perfect confusion and everybody was bringing suggestions'. Apparently unsure of how to proceed, the US Government did what all administrative bodies do in such circumstances and formed a committee, seeming more than happy to have experienced businessmen take over the expansion of the air services on their behalf.

The Joint Army and Navy Technical Board, which was formed on 5 May 1917, was intended to formulate the proposed aeroplane building programme and to establish which designs were to be built. Although the members of this board were, at least in theory, the most knowledgeable officers available from the two forces, it was a purely advisory body, without any real authority or power, and it simply passed suggestions onto the War Department via a number of other civilian boards and commissions. The most important of these, with regard to the aeroplane building programme, was the Aircraft Production Board, which first met on 16 May 1917, some six weeks after America's entry into the war, after being created by a resolution of the Council of National Defense, which authorised the new board to carry out the following roles:

1. To co-operate with the plane and engine design department of the army and navy, and with manufacturers and engineering laboratories to advance the science of aviation, and to stimulate the production of a better type of aircraft.
2. To advise and assist in standardization of material and parts.
3. To investigate the source of supply of aircraft and the materials entering into them, with a view to co-ordination of designs of all aircraft matters through the officers of the allied countries stationed here: arrangements with existing American factories as to the kinds

of aircraft best suited to their organisations and facilities; suitable arrangement when necessary to advance government funds or to make arrangements on a cost plus basis, and utilization of idle facilities and creation of new sources of supply as in the judgement of the board may be necessary.

4. To co-operate with the inspection organisations of the army and navy.
5. Following the selection of sites for aviation schools and supply sites, by the military departments, to advise in regard to buying or leasing the land, preparing it for use, and erecting all buildings.
6. To advise regarding priority of material deliveries as between the departments.

Although again purely an advisory body, the advice given by this board was generally followed by the Government, almost without question, perhaps due to the strength of character of its members. Its chairman, appointed by the Council of National Defense, was Howard E. Coffin, Vice-President and formerly Chief Engineer of the Hudson Motor Car Company, who was known as 'the father of standardisation' for his role in encouraging automobile manufacturers to share their patents. He was also a governor of the Aero Club of America, and had been Chairman of the Pre-war Industrial Preparedness Committee, which had produced an inventory of factories capable of making munitions should the need arise. Already a millionaire, he was one of the members of the Wall Street syndicate that had invested in both Curtiss and Wright-Martin. During 1916, he said that 'the problems confronting the aircraft industry are wonderfully simple compared to those of the automobile industry'. This was probably referring to the comparative lack of competition and the freedom from the obligation to produce a new model every year just to stimulate public interest, which had already become an established requirement for American car makers. His salary, as Chairman of the Aircraft Production Board, was a nominal $1 a year.

Coffin then appointed Sidney D. Waldon, Edward A. Deeds, and Robert L. Montgomery as civilian members. Chief Signal Officer General George O. Squier represented the US Army and Admiral David W. Taylor represented the US Navy.

With mass production very much in mind, the civilians each had backgrounds and experience associated with volume production industries, although none had experience of aeroplane manufacture.

Deeds was an engineer, inventor, and industrialist who, after studying electrical engineering at Cornell University, began work at the Thresher Company in Dayton, Ohio, moving to the National Cash Register Company, which shared the same building. In 1899, he oversaw the electrification of the building before turning his attention to applying electric power to the company's products. This gave NCR such prominence that new factories were opened in Canada and throughout Europe, but in 1913, along with twenty-six other NCR executives, he was convicted of violating the Anti-Trust Act and was sentenced to one year's imprisonment, but managed to have the conviction overturned on appeal.

During 1909, his friend and associate Charles F. Kettering invented an electric starter for car engines, developing and perfecting it in a workshop housed in Deeds' barn. Together, he and Deeds formed the Dayton Engineering Laboratories Company (Delco), selling starters and ignition systems and so establishing Deeds' links with the automobile industry. In 1915, Deeds left NCR, working full time at the ever-expanding Delco, although he would return to NCR later in his career. He also co-founded the Engineers Club of Dayton and was a keen amateur astronomer.

Robert Montgomery's business expertise was in corporate finance and banking, while Sidney Waldon was an Englishman who immigrated to America in 1892, when he was nineteen years old. He became a vice-president and general manager of the Packard Motor Car Company, then America's foremost manufacturer of luxury automobiles. An enthusiastic supporter of early aviation, he helped organise air races and similar events.

Sidney Dunn Walden was a key figure in America's Aircraft Production Programme.

Then, on 24 May 1917, President Woodrow Wilson received a cable from Alexandre Ribot, the Prime Minister of France, whose army was almost on the point of revolt and was clearly in need of the assurance of future support, in which he stated:

> It is desired that in order to co-operate with the French Aeronautics the American Government should adopt the following program; The formation of a Flying Corps of 4,500 aeroplanes to be sent to the French front during the campaign of 1918 The total number of pilots, including reserve, should be 5,000 and 50,000 mechanicians.
>
> 2,000 planes should be constructed each month, as well as 4,000 engines, by the American factories, this is to say that during the first six months of 1918 16,500 aeroplane (of the last type), and 30,000 engines will have to be built. The French Government is anxious to know if the American Government accepts this proposition, which would allow the allies to win supremacy of the air.

Supremacy of the air had yet to be obtained by either side, Allied or German, although superiority had switched from side to side as better aeroplanes were introduced. Both had started the war with relatively small fleets of unarmed aeroplanes, and had operated in almost friendly rivalry above the trenches until the introduction of the synchronised machine gun in the summer of 1915, which had given Germany the upper hand. New Allied fighters that came into service during 1916 had addressed the balance until the spring of 1917, when Germany's newest fighters again gave her superiority and resulted in 'Bloody April'; during this single month, the British RFC lost over 30 per cent of its front-line aircraft, making regaining parity an immediate concern to the Allies and making overall supremacy an ideal goal.

The General Staff were in immediate support of Ribot's proposal, even though this required America to build, in one year, a larger and more powerful air force than France, with an already established aeroplane industry, had been able to do in three years. On 29 May, the Joint Army and Navy Technical Board met to consider it and reported to the Secretaries of the Army and Navy:

> The French Government, on May 24, 1917 requested the United States Government to cooperate with the French Aeronautics, and form a flying corps of 4,500 airplanes, personnel and material; such a flying corps to be available for active service in France during the spring campaign of 1918.
>
> To meet the foregoing request, the needs of the United States Army for service airplanes and engines, to be used in Europe, are as indicated:

| | | |
|---|---|---|
| Reconnaissance & Artillery Control | 3,000 | with 1,000 in reserve |
| Fighting | 5,000 | with 1,667 in reserve |
| Bombing | 1,000 | with 333 in reserve |

> In order that the United States Government may meet the request of the French Government, immediate steps should be taken to start manufacture, in the United States, of the above airplanes.

Howard Coffin, Chairman of the Aircraft Production Board, thought that this programme was only capable of accomplishment if the funds were made available within thirty days, that definite instruction was given to proceed within the same period, and that no delays, for whatever reason, were permitted. Coffin presumably thought that the types of aeroplanes to be produced, which had yet to be specified, would be decided by the Joint Army and Navy Technical Board and specified in the 'definite instruction to proceed'.

Secretary of War Newton D. Baker, in support of the plan, told Congress that it 'lives up to America's tradition of doing things on a grand scale'. The plan appealed to America's national pride and so gained almost immediate approval. Speaking at a luncheon in New York on 8 June, Coffin said: 'America's great opportunity lies before her. The Road to Berlin lies through the air. The eagle must end this war'.

It is obvious that air power was widely seen as America's opportunity to show off her industrial strength and so take her rightful place on the world stage.

As time between overhauls was, in those days, very short, a spare engine was required for each machine. This meant that twice as many engines as aeroplanes would need to be built, a task America's automobile industry felt well able to undertake, after all, the current production of automobile engines, from all manufacturers, was in excess of 100,000 units each month and this programme called for an average of just 5,000, albeit much larger, units per month.

Aeroplane production and the expansion of the Aeronautical Services thus became America's flagship programme, the centrepiece of her mobilisation plans, and the focus of media attention, although it was not without opposition and doubt; General Kohn, Commanding the War College, thought that the plan could never be achieved within the proposed time scale, but also thought that whatever the programme did produce could only do good. He stated: 'If it fails at least we will have done something'.

3

# The US Standardised Aero Engine

In Europe, aero engines seemed to take almost twice as long to develop, from concept to production, as did aeroplanes, but often reached obsolescence almost as soon. This was due to the ever-constant demand for ever more power, in order to produce ever better performance. Additionally, there was a considerable diversity of design, with over thirty different types in production in England alone—a situation the recently appointed Director General of Aircraft Production Sir William Weir was trying to address. He concentrated orders for future production onto fewer types, hoping to improve overall output, which had hitherto never been able to keep pace with demand.

Engines built by different companies, ostensibly to the same design, often differed so much in detail so that the parts were not interchangeable between them. The Hispano-Suiza V8, for example, was manufactured both as a direct drive unit and with a reduction gear, with differing manufacturers producing different gear ratios, driving different propellers, and requiring different parts. Although some effort was made to keep the engines in use within any one unit to a similar make and model, it made stores keeping administration and logistics all far more difficult tasks than they need have been.

Edward Deeds therefore thought that America should apply itself to producing an engine of sufficiently high power to remain in use for some years, without the need for constant development. Additionally, it would have to be straightforward, if not simple, to manufacture in quantity, while having the greatest possible interchangeability of parts. Immediately after the French proposals had been adopted, the wheels were put in motion to bring this about.

These views were shared by Jesse G. Vincent, a vice-president of the Packard Motor Car Company. Vincent, a natural born designer who had learned engineering largely by taking correspondence courses, had started work at the Burroughs Adding Machine Company in Detroit before joining the Hudson Motor Car Company in 1910, replacing Coffin—who had just been appointed as a vice-president—as Chief Engineer. Vincent stayed two years at Hudson before moving on to a similar position at Packard, where he would remain for the rest of his career.

On 29 May 1917, Vincent arrived in Washington at the request of Deeds. There he met Elbert J. Hall, the designer at the Hall-Scott Company, whose aero engines were then the most advanced in production in the US. The two engineers were given a suite of rooms at the famous Willard Hotel on Pennsylvania Avenue and the assistance of a team of draughtsmen, and were instructed to produce, as soon as possible, a design for an aero engine specifically intended for ease of manufacture by plants already existing within the US. They were also provided with the details and, where available, the blueprints of many of the engines currently in use by both sides in Europe.

The new engine was initially named the 'U.S. Standardized Aero Engine' until patriotic fervour renamed it the 'Liberty'. The plan was to produce a standard design that could be built in four-, six-, eight-, or twelve-cylinder versions to provide a range of engines to meet all requirements. This meant adopting separate cylinders, a design style that had been already rendered obsolescent by the monoblock design of the Hispano-Suiza and its derivatives, but which made for ease of manufacture, especially by mass production methods. On 31 May, the two engineers produced a preliminary report including the proposed range of engines, with predictions of power outputs and weights, and were advised that the eight- and twelve-cylinder versions were the most needed, as other engines already in production within the US adequately covered the lower outputs.

A cylinder bore of 5 inches and a stroke of 7 inches was decided upon as being largely in line with common practice, and within the manufacturing capacity available. This gave a swept volume of 137 cubic inches (2.25 litres) per cylinder. As the engine was to be direct drive, thereby eliminating the weight and complication of reduction gearing, its rotation speed was of necessity limited to a less than 2,000 rpm, beyond which a propeller became inefficient. A propeller rotational speed of around between 1,500 and 1,800 rpm was then usual practice; at this speed, an engine power output of around 12–15 hp per litre was the norm and so it was predicted that a V8 version would produce around 225 hp and the V12 around 350 hp, which was considered to be ideal to meet the demands of current aeroplane designs.

Working with commendable despatch, the two engineers produced a detailed design just five days after first meeting, simply by combining elements of well-proven practice together with some preliminary designs already prepared by Hall-Scott. The basic cylinder design, already in use in some Hall-Scott engines, was similar to those currently used by Mercedes, Rolls-Royce, and Lorraine Deitrich. The camshaft and valve mechanism were copied from Mercedes and its drive system from Hall-Scott. The pistons were also based on those of the successful Hall-Scott engines, as was the propeller hub design; the crankshaft followed common practice, and the blade and fork connecting rods were as used both by De-Dion and Cadillac car engines, among others. The water and oil pumps followed Packard design and a carburettor was developed by the Zenith Carburettor Company. A more detailed technical description of the design is given in Appendix I.

However, in two respects, the design departed from accepted practice. Firstly, the angle between the cylinder banks, for both V8 and V12 versions, was set at 45 degrees, instead of the normal 90 and 60 degrees respectively—these being the angles through which the crankshaft turned between each individual cylinder's firing. Preserving this angle between firing stokes meant that the geometry of the piston, connecting rod, and crankpin always formed the most advantageous angle at the point when the pressure created by igniting the charge of mixture in the cylinder was

A preserved example of the eight cylinder Liberty engine, a variant that, although successful, never entered volume production as other engines of similar power were already available.

at its highest, thereby producing the greatest possible torque. Although selecting this angle reduced the engine's frontal area, thereby allowing for a more streamlined cowling, and also stiffened the crankcase, it also meant that the power, and especially the torque, produced was a little reduced from what might otherwise have been possible, and that the smooth running of the engine was slightly impaired.

The second departure from normal practice was the adoption of an automobile-style coil ignition system rather than the magneto typical of aero engines, as special system being developed by Delco to fire twin sparking plugs in a V12 engine. This change from standard practice conveniently side-stepped America's current lack of capacity to manufacture magnetos, while its automobile industry was familiar with coil ignition systems.

On 4 June, after approval by the Joint Technical Board, orders were placed for five examples each of the V8 and V12 versions to be built by Packard for testing. The sum of $250,000 was apportioned from Signal Corps' funds to finance the building of these prototypes. The definitive layout drawings were submitted to the Bureau of Standards, for approval

Maj. H. H. Arnold standing alongside the first example of the V12 Liberty engine. Working under Col. William 'Billy' Mitchell, Arnold supervised the expansion of the America's air services during the First World War and rose to command them immediately prior to the Second World War. (*US Air Force Photo*)

while the individual component drawings needed to facilitate manufacture were produced at Packard under the direction of Mr O. E. Hunt.

Parts for these first engines were made by a number of companies from across the US, including the following: Aluminium Casting Co. (Cleveland, Ohio), pistons; Burd High Compression Ring Co. (Rockford, Illinois), piston rings; Cadillac Motor Car Co. (Detroit, Michigan), connecting rods and rocker assemblies; General Aluminium Manufacturing Co. (Detroit, Michigan), bearings; Gibson Company (Muskegon, Mich), springs; L. O. Gordon Manufacturing Co. (Muskegon, Michigan), camshafts; Hall-Scott (Berkeley, California), bevel gears; Hess-Bright Manufacturing (Philadelphia, Pennsylvania), ball bearings; and Park Drop Forge Co. (Cleveland, Ohio), crankshaft casting.

Packard produced all the other parts, as well as making patterns for the castings, machining the crankshaft, and carrying out the final assembly.

The first example completed, a prototype V8, was shipped to Washington on an express train accompanied by engineers from Packard—legend stating that they were still frantically working on it—and was handed over to the Bureau of Standards on 3 July, fulfilling the promise to have it delivered by Independence Day. However, although this event was, as might be expected, well publicised, this engine was never run and it appears to have been produced simply to confirm the design.

Testing of a completed engine began at the Packard plant on 21 July, when 'working in' was carried out by coupling the engine to an external power source to keep it turning over before the engine was first started the following day. Within days, it had been run for eight hours non-stop both on a test rig and then fitted with a propeller. At one point, the water supply was disconnected and the temperature allowed to reach boiling point to check that no steam pockets occurred. It was then taken to Washington and demonstrated, first to the Bureau of Standards on the evening of 31 July and then to the Joint Army and Navy Board the following afternoon, when it ran perfectly from 4.30 p.m. until 6 p.m., using only one quart of oil, which was considered very frugal for the time.

The V12 version soon followed, beginning dynamometer tests on 13 August, and although the carburettor had to be replaced and the intake manifold modified before it would run smoothly, by 17 August, it was producing 346 hp at 1,800 rpm. By 25 August, it had completed an officially observed fifty-hour test, producing an average of 315 hp at 1,584 rpm. After this test, it was stripped down and examined for any wear and found to be in good condition, with only slight wear evident on the pistons and cylinder bores. Some further modification of the intake manifold and a new type of small end bearing were, however, recommended, after which the engine was approved for production.

On 29 August, a Liberty engine made its first flight when a specially built LWF aeroplane, fitted with V8 No. 3, took off from Buffalo, New York, piloted by a Mr Blakely. Further tests followed, largely to adjust the carburation, and the next day, the machine was taken up by an army pilot, Major Kilner, who was impressed with its power. Flight testing of the V12 began in October, when three more hand-built prototypes were delivered from Packard, the first flight being made on 21 October in a Curtiss flying boat of the US Navy. On 28 October, the engine made its first flight fitted in a D.H.4 airframe, which had been shipped over from England.

Testing and development, initially of the hand-built prototypes, continued throughout the remainder of the year and on into 1918, when production examples finally began to become available.

Members of the Buick Motor Company's senior management pose with a Liberty engine. Their apparent pride was justified as, in addition to aiding the war effort, building the Liberty was good for the company's profits.

4

# Preliminary Proposals

Following America's acceptance, in principle, of the programme requested by the French, the Joint Army and Navy Technical Aircraft Board drew its own plans. On 29 May, just five days after the arrival of Ribot's telegram (which proposed the production of 12,000 aeroplanes and 24,000 engines during the first six months of 1918), their proposal was submitted to and approved by the Secretaries of War and the Navy.

Next, Howard Coffin's Aircraft Production Board—and after consulting with various manufacturing companies—prepared a preliminary production programme. By 13 June 1917, it had listed the aeroplanes it proposed should be built and the companies that should build them. The report's rather terse prose style reflected the urgency with which it had been prepared:

> 5,000 Curtiss JN-4 Training Machines
> Planned to use the existing factories as far as practicable including Curtiss up to Jan. 1st and to create new sources between now and Jan. 1st that will be able to meet the demands thereafter. Present plans estimate a shortage of training planes during first 120 days, an output of approximately 2,000 prior to Jan. 1st and 3000 from Jan. 1st to July 1st 1918. Two sources of supply for the Curtiss OX-5 engine and two sources for the Hall-Scott A7A engine.
>
> This program is already under way.
>
> 2,500 DH4 Reconnaissance Machines for Advanced Training
> English Air Board have offered to ship a sample plane which has already been cabled for. This will save some time in preparation for manufacture. Expect to expand Standard Aero and L-W-F-Engineering and to create two other new sources of supply with common sources for fittings

The Curtiss JN-4, which was already in production when war was declared, was the Aircraft Production Board's selection as a primary trainer.

A British-built D.H.4, powered by a Rolls-Royce Eagle engine, in service with the RFC as a day bomber.

and forgings. Planning to use Rolls-Royce 250 HP engines built in the Pierce-Arrow factory in 500 of these planes and the balance to take the U.S.12-A engine. Expect to have 2500 complete planes and 500 spare engines by July 1, 1918.

800 S.E.5 Pursuit planes for Advanced Training
Wright-Martin Co. now building the 150 HP Hispano-Suiza engine for the French Government. Will be through about August and reach production of about twenty per day by Jan. 1st 1918. On U.S. order Wright-Martin have offered to build an eastern plant with a capacity of 100 to 125 planes per month, which would fill this order. Geo. H. Houston, formerly Gen. Mgr, of Curtiss is now V.Pres. And Gen. Mgr. of the Wright-Martin Co.

Have cabled for a sample of this machine and the Air Board have agreed to release it.

800 S.P.A.D. Pursuit planes for Advanced Training.
This takes 150 Hispano-Suiza motor which is already in production in this country. Planes to be built by the Fisher Body Corporation of Detroit following the production of 500 training machines.

This company is making 1,100 open bodies and 200 limousines every day and has an organisation already selected to take hold of airplane production on as large a scale as necessary.

The Royal Aircraft Factory's highly successful S.E.5 fighter. Over 5,000 were built, all powered by variants of the V8 Hispano-Suiza engine. It performed very well in active service, but the US originally selected it as an advanced trainer.

800 Sopwith Pursuit planes for Rotary Engine Training
This takes 130 HP Clerget engine which cannot be in production before Feb. 15 1918. Plan would be to bring General Vehicle Co. (now building rotary engines), General Electric Co., Brewster & Co., who are building the English Daimler engine and possibly the Laval Turbine Co.

Thomas Morse Airplane Co. at Ithaca, N.Y. is being given rotary engined plane work in anticipation of this probable demand.

Curtiss R.4 and R-6—Land and Sea Reconnaissance
Engines are now made at separate factory devoted exclusively to one type. Orders should be given to Curtiss upon conditions that two new sources of supply are created for their manufacture, preferably in Rochester and Cleveland, where supervision can readily be given from Buffalo.

175 Farman Seaplanes
This uses the Hispano-Suiza engine which is in production here. Would recommend that Burgess and Aeromarine build and assemble 125 planes and that Verville Co. build and assemble 50 planes.

12,000 Fighting, Bombing, Artillery Control & Reconnaissance Machines
Instead of attempting to duplicate the various types of French fighting machines it is proposed to concentrate on the Sopwith as outlined above, using the rotary motor built by the General Vehicle Company, and on the S.P.A.D utilizing the Hispano-Suiza engine which is now in production.

Another type of fighting machine will also be developed utilizing the U.S.8 A motor as soon as possible.

We will concentrate on the Reconnaissance and Artillery Control types relieving French factories of heavy production of these types. This will permit them to concentrate on the fighting types utilizing the rotary engine. In the meantime the rotary engine production will be materially increased in this country.

With the U.S.8A and U.S.12A in quantity production before January 1st and the Lorraine Deitrich by March 1, 1918, we can meet the increased reconnaissance and artillery control program.

With designs from Europe on or before August 1st it will be possible to have planes in November from Curtiss and in December and January from sources of supply established to make training machines, but switched over to these as training orders are transferred to other new sources of supply. The output of these planes will temporarily exceed that of engines.

> It is estimated that production of these types will have to reach and hold 1800 per month by March 1918. The Curtiss Company have estimated that they can reach an output of 30 per day, or 750 per month of pursuit of fighting machines by January 1st 1918. We expect to have at least two other sources of supply equal in size and capacity to the Curtiss Company and to mobilize the productive capacities for wood working of some centers like Grand Rapids, Amesbury, Philadelphia, and Camden, Cincinnati, Syracuse, Kansas City and St. Louis.

Coffin's report went on to describe, in a similarly terse style, how the work would be assigned to various factories, including Dayton-Wright, which, along with Fisher Body, would eventually play a key role in the final programme. He then went on to explain the Aircraft Production Board's suggested plans for the construction of the engines necessary to power all these aeroplanes, concentrating, of course, on the US Standardised design, of which he said:

> These motors are being designed to suit American practice and quantity production. While we feel this is the most important single element in our program we are not relying entirely upon it, but are closely following the engine developments of individual companies here and will of course plan to put the best European engine designs as selected by the Joint Army & Navy Technical Board into earliest possible production.
>
> Utilizing the automobile industry has the advantage that it will probably be least interfered with by other munitions work. It will not require new plants or equipment, but will require the taking over of whatever portion of the various plants necessary to meet the demands and thereby reduce the output of pleasure vehicle proportionately. We are certain from the temper of this industry that any sacrifice of regular business necessary to meet the emergency will be willingly and cooperatively made.
>
> The quantities of raw materials are comparatively small and will not conflict with demands in other lines.

There followed a statement to the effect that there were 114 companies in the National Automobile Chamber of Commerce, all accustomed to the strenuous manufacturing conditions imposed by the need to introduce an annual change of model. A list was then made of those the Board were considering engaging to assist in carrying out its engine building programme, presumably after some consultation with their respective managements.

Aware that the production of training machines, and then the training of the crews, must come before any operations could begin, the proposed programme broadly followed the timescale stated in the French Premier's telegram; it was planned for 1 July 1918 to be the start date for operations in France. Coffin's report therefore stated:

> We believe that the Aircraft Production Board can arrange for the production during the next 12 months of an engine for every plane and at least a spare engine for every five planes. The deficit in spare engines for training machines will be made up during the spring and the deficit in engines for combat machines will be made up during the summer of 1918.

It ended on a confident note, confirming that 'the program as submitted to the Aircraft production Board is a gigantic one but capable of accomplishment as outlined provided funds are quickly appropriated and no delays are permitted'.

Coffin also took pains to assure the Board of Munitions that the aircraft building programme would have no adverse effect on the production of trucks, artillery shells, or any other commodity vital to the war effort, especially as it largely employed different materials and methods from other armament manufacture.

In selecting the types of machine listed, the Board had clearly taken note of the French suggestion that the planes should be 'of the last type' as those selected—not just for operational use, but even as advanced trainers—were types only just being introduced by America's allies. The D.H.4 had first entered service in March 1917, and the S.E.5 the following month. While the report does not actually specify which model of Sopwith it was planned to build, the reference to a 130-hp Clerget engine confirms that this was the Camel, the first examples of which were only just coming into action.

The suggestions of the French Premier's cable, although taken as a model for America's expanded air services, had been carefully evaluated along with America's own plan, which called for the production of only 12,000 combat types, rather than the 16,500 suggested by Ribot. However, the total number required was greater as it included training machines, which the French had ignored.

Contemporaneously with the preparation of the aircraft building programme, similar steps were being taken to prepare for the expansion of the Aeronautical Section, with new airfields being constructed and training schools established, all based closely on the training system already in use by other countries. In France, a small group of officers, under the command of Major William Mitchell, began the establishment of a headquarters in Paris. From this location, operations could be directed in readiness for the eventual arrival of the aeroplanes and their crews.

5

# The Mission to Europe

Although the preliminary production programme that had been prepared early in June 1917 detailed precisely what types of training machines it was planned that America should build, and which companies should build them, the types of machines intended for front-line service still had yet to be decided upon. Advisors had arrived from Europe, but understandably, they often offered conflicting opinions, each considering their own company, or own nation's, products as superior to all others, and so leaving America still uncertain of which types were most likely to be most suited to combat operations the following year. The essence of the problem was that if they were to select models that were already proving a success in service then given the speed with which aerial warfare was developing, these could, and almost certainly would, be obsolete before America could get them into production, and into action; whereas, if they selected new designs that had yet to prove themselves in action, these could easily turn out to be a disappointment. The ideal solution would be to select designs that were just entering service, and already proving highly satisfactory, with the potential to continue to be so for some time to come. This was a task that was very much easier to say than to do as rapid advances continued to be made by both sides, sometimes rendering new designs almost instantly obsolete and limiting the life span of even the most successful designs.

The French High Commission in Washington DC had already made it clear that, despite being allies in a common cause, royalty payments would still be demanded for each and every example of a French design manufactured in quantity by America, a position that America viewed almost as taxing her for entering the war, even though such payments were common in Europe when one company was contracted to build the designs of another.

Instead, America took the more liberal view that there should be a free exchange of information between the Allied nations. However, in order to expedite progress, America proposed one-off royalty payments of $100,000 each for up to three designs of aeroplanes, and three types of engine, if these were adopted for production in America. Some discussions had previously taken place, but with the relevant parties some 3,000 miles apart, separated by five or six time zones, and often speaking different languages, progress was understandably slow.

America therefore decided that the best solution would be to send representatives to visit their allies in Europe and thus collect the required information first hand, arrange for engineering drawings and sample aircraft to be shipped to the US, and to negotiate face to face with officials in Britain and France over patent rights and royalty payments.

Major Raynal Cawthorne Bolling was chosen to lead the Aeronautical Commission to Europe, acting as the representative of Secretary of War Newton D. Baker. Bolling was therefore appointed to the Aircraft Production Board expressly for that purpose. For convenience, this commission is therefore often referred to simply as 'The Bolling Mission'.

Raynal Bolling, who had graduated from Harvard Law School in 1902, had previously worked both for a law practice and in industry as legal advisor to the United States Steel Corporation. He had learned to fly in 1915 and had accepted a commission in the New York National Guard, first forming, and then commanding, the first Air Detachment to become fully established, possessing both aeroplanes and the pilots to fly them. When America entered the war, Bolling was immediately called to active service, and began preparing legal documents in connection with the appropriate of funding for the Aeronautical Section, Signal Corps. He was selected to lead the mission to Europe largely because of his wealth of experience and considerable skill in negotiating prices, royalty agreements, and similar contractual details.

Assigned to assist him were Maj. Robert Glendinning, ASSC; Capt. Virginius E. Clark, ASSC; Capt. Edgar S. Gorrell, ASSC; Commander G. C. Westervelt, US Navy; Lt W. G. Childs, US Navy; Mr Howard C. Marmon, Nordyke & Marmon Co.; Mr Herbert Hughes, Packard Motor Co.; Mr C. H. Hailman, Northway Motor Co.; Mr W. B. Hurley, Midvale Steel Co.; Mr R. A. Vail, Dodge Motor Corp; and Mr Stay, Aluminum Casting Co.

Two of the US Army officers, Clark and Gorrell, were engineers who had graduated from the Massachusetts Institute of Technology, Gorrell as a Master of Science. Westervelt was the US Navy's aeronautical expert and Childs was a specialist in engines. Hailman and Hurley were metallurgists, and Vail was an efficiency expert and production engineer.

Raynal Bolling dressed in flying clothing while serving with the National Guard before America's entry into the war.

Maj. Glendinning had been a banker and was expected to assist in financial negotiations, while Mr Hughes had, until recently, been in charge of Packard's Paris office and so already knew many of the leading engineers in Europe.

Associated with the mission, although not actually part of it, were a group of ninety-three skilled workers and foreman, including forge and foundry men, tool designers, pattern makers, and draughtsmen, selected from companies mostly connected with the automobile industry, in Detroit, Indianapolis, Buffalo, and Long Island, under the leadership of a Mr R. I. Mowry. These skilled men were being sent to Europe to be placed in factories for a month or two so as to learn how things were done there, to pick up tips that were never made entirely clear by documents and drawings, and generally to learn anything and everything that might assist in fulfilling America's production plans. They sailed from New York, aboard the steamship *St Paul* of the American Line, on 16 June 1917. Although over twenty years old, the 11,000-ton *St Paul* was fairly fast, usually making the Atlantic crossing in six days, its speed helping reduce the ever-present risk of its being torpedoed by a German submarine. Their safe arrival was described in the British aviation press along with an acerbic comment that if these American 'experts' were anything like their British counterparts, then production in America would probably progress better in their absence.

Raynal Bolling was given confidential orders in a letter from the Adjutant General, headed 'Detail Abroad' and dated 9 June 1917, in which he was instructed to proceed to Paris, via London, for temporary duty in connection with the Air Services and to report to the chief signal officer there. The other army officers received their orders to accompany and assist Maj. Bolling in a letter from the Chief Signal Officer dated 11 June.

Howard Coffin, chairman of the Aircraft Production Board, sent his own letter to Bolling, offering almost superfluous advice: 'Get all the facts before making a decision, and remember our motto is "Vite"'.

Bolling and his companions embarked on the White Star Line steamship RMS *Adriatic* during the afternoon of Saturday 16 June 1917, in readiness for its sailing the following morning. During the voyage, they passed the time in technical discussions, pooling their knowledge as far as possible in preparation for their mission. Also on board the *Adriatic* was Maj. Tulsanne, a member of the French mission to the USA who was returning home and who was able to assist Bolling's party by teaching them some basic French words and phrases.

The *Adriatic* docked at Liverpool early on the morning of 26 June, the members of the mission travelling to London by express train the same day and arriving there in the afternoon. While in London, Maj. Bolling,

The RMS *Adriatic*, aboard which the Bolling Mission sailed for Europe on 17 June 1917.

as the appointed representative of Secretary of War Newton D. Baker and thus of the US Government, spent a great deal of time in negotiations with members of British Air Board, usually accompanied by Gorrell and sometimes by Marmon too. The topics discussed, and eventually agreed upon, included securing an adequate supply of linen, with which aeroplanes were then usually covered, over which some misunderstanding had evolved, with Peter Fletcher being appointed to represent the US in all future discussion concerning the supply of this vital material. Ways in which America could supply scarce materials to Britain were also agreed, including meeting a requirement for an improved supply of ball bearings. Arrangements were also made, by Bolling, for the training of American flyers in schools both in England and in Canada.

The question of royalty payments to manufacturers whose designs were adopted for production by America was also discussed, with the American Ambassador Mr Page joining Bolling in meetings with Lord Cowdray, President of the Air Board, who then conveyed their conclusions to Prime Minister David Lloyd George.

Meanwhile, the other mission members engaged in discussion, mostly of a technical nature, with aeroplane manufacturers, who agreed to despatch all the drawings and samples, both of completed aeroplanes and engines as requested, with all possible haste, on the understanding that these would not be copied until the question of royalty payments was finally resolved. Despatch began almost before the delegates had left England, all shipments being completed by the end of July.

In accordance with Coffin's instruction, it was a fairly brief visit, the whole mission departing for France after less than a week in England on Tuesday 2 July. They had arranged for several sample aeroplanes—including a Bristol Scout, Bristol F.2B Fighter, Sopwith Camel, and a Royal Aircraft Factory S.E.5—to be shipped to the US along with engineering drawings and technical specifications. A sample D.H.4 had already been requested prior to the mission's arrival in Europe.

Bolling and Gorrell were taken by aeroplane from Dover to the RFC Depot at St Omer, and then by car to Paris, where they were soon joined by the rest of the group who had travelled more conventionally—by boat and train. The party of skilled workers followed them to France a few days later, leaving about a third of their number behind to continue their exchange of information with their English counterparts in various factories around the country.

On 3 July, Maj. Bolling, observing strict military protocol, reported to Gen. Pershing, commander of the US Army in Europe, before proceeding with his negotiations with the French authorities. These covered similar ground to those in England, but with the added difficulties both of the

A D.H.4 in flight. A sample was ordered by the Bolling Mission while in England and was delivered to America in July, while the mission was still in Europe.

language problem and the political situation in France at the time. For his first two meetings with the French Ministry, Bolling was accompanied by the US Ambassador to help to pave the way. The French Air Minister M. Vincent attended some of the meetings, but mostly left the discussions to his deputy, M. Flandin.

The French had their own agenda for the discussions, attempting to convince Bolling that the US should immediately place orders with French manufacturers for the 20,000 aeroplanes and 30,000 engines to fulfil their Prime Minister's proposal, while Bolling was seeking to obtain licences to build any French designs selected for production in the US. It was finally agreed that America would purchase 5,000 fighter aeroplanes from France, to equip its front-line squadrons until American-built machines became available, and that samples of the aeroplanes and engines the mission considered suitable for building in America, together with all necessary details to facilitate their manufacture, would be shipped to the US as soon as possible. With this compromise reached, negotiations to draw up the necessary formal contracts began.

Meanwhile, the Italian authorities pressured the mission to extend their visit to include Italy before returning home, and eventually Bolling was persuaded to go, his orders being suitably amended by HQ AEF on 12 July. Mr Vail was left in Paris to continue negotiations, along with several of the other mission members, while the remainder of the party of skilled workers remained distributed among French factories to carry out their own role there.

Bolling, accompanied by Clark, Gorrell, Westervelt, Childs, Marmon, and Hughes, left Paris at 8.25 p.m. on Sunday 15 July by train, arriving at Modane, close to the Italian border, the next morning. Here they were joined by Italian guides and conveyed by car through the mountains to Turin, where they inspected an airfield and watched a flying display staged on their behalf by the most noted Italian pilots. On 19 July, in Milan, the party visited a large military camp and several factories, including that of the Caproni Company before being entertained by the Chamber of Commerce, the other guests including both Signor Giovanni Caproni and his brother, Dr Caproni.

This pattern was repeated in Genoa and then at the Flying School at Malpensa. On 21 July, Bolling, Clark, and Gorrell were flown in Caproni machines to Campoformido to rejoin the rest of the party who had travelled there by train. They then went on to the headquarters of the Italian Army, where they witnessed a parade for the presentation of medals. Further visits to both airfields and factories followed, along with a visit to Venice. During their time in Italy, they were also taken to a section of the front to see the flying services in action. Many of these activities were not directly concerned with the purpose of the mission, but nonetheless, arrangements were eventually made for some sample aeroplanes to be shipped to America as soon as possible for further evaluation.

The American were treated, throughout their entire time in Italy, like visiting royalty, and were not allowed to spend any money, even on personal items such as postcards or souvenirs, all of which were paid for by the Italian Government.

The Bolling Mission left Turin by train at 6 p.m. on 26 July. They travelled back to Paris, returning first to their previous quarters at a hotel on the Champs Elysee before moving around the corner to 45 Avenue Montaigne, where Lt-Col. Mitchell had his headquarters.

Bolling was disappointed to discover that although the French had faithfully promised before his departure for Italy to ship the sample aeroplanes, which included two Breguets, a SPAD, and a Nieuport, to America immediately, nothing had yet been done. He made renewed efforts to expedite their despatch.

Bolling's report recommended building the Caproni Triplane as America's heavy bomber.

The Bregeut 14 was bought from the French as a reconnaissance and bombing machine for use until American-built aircraft could be shipped to France. However, the production shortfall meant that it stayed in service until the end of the war

Meanwhile, the contract with the French Government for the supply of 5,000 aeroplanes was finally completed. It was signed by Bolling on 30 July. Under its terms, France was to supply suitable machines to equip the US Air Service until aeroplanes manufactured in America could reach Europe; in return, the US were to send over both raw materials and machine tools to aid France's own munitions production programme.

The aeroplanes to be supplied by France were 1,500 Breguet two seaters (for both Corps work and bombing); 2,000 SPAD fighters, each with a spare 200-hp Hispano-Suiza engine; and 1,500 SPADs, or Nieuports, each with a spare 150-hp Gnome rotary engine.

Its tasks thus completed, the majority of the party then returned, firstly to England, and from there to the US. However, Bolling, along with Glendinning, Gorrell, and Hughes, remained in Paris to take up new duties there.

Although the key points regarding the agreements achieved during the Mission's tour of Europe had already been conveyed to Washington by letter and by cable as events occurred and decisions were reached, and individual mission members would each report on their own activities, Bolling spent some time preparing a lengthy report of every aspect of the mission. It was addressed, in accordance with his original orders, to the Chief Signal Officer of the Army General George O. Squier.

Maj. Bolling completed his report on 15 August, and in it, he confirmed 1 July 1918 as the pivotal date before which America could make little or no contribution to the war in the air. He also described his experiences in Europe, and explained the decisions reached. The relevant passages are as follows:

> ROYALTIES OR RIGHTS TO MANUFACTURE IN AMERICA.—The principle with respect to this matter adopted by the Aircraft Production Board and the United States Government before we left America was that there should be free exchange of all such rights among the Allied nations for the duration of the war. The only exception to this rule was the arrangement made by the Aircraft Production Board with the French High Commission in Washington respecting the payment to the French Government of $100,000 each for three types of airplanes and three types of motors thought to be immediately desirable in America. This exception was specifically stated not to be in derogation of the general principle established.
>
> On reaching England, I announced the position of the United States Government to the British Air Board and it was discussed between us at length and in detail. It was deemed of such importance in its industrial and political aspects that I was informed it must be laid before Mr Lloyd

George and the Cabinet; but the British Air Board recognised the broad equities of the position taken by the United States. After our numerous conferences, I was informed that the British Government accepted the principle presented by the United States, assumed all responsibility to the British manufacturers and agreed that the United States during the duration of the war might manufacture or cause to be manufactured all types of British airplanes and engines recommended and adopted for quantity production in the United States.

In France the situation in respect to this matter was and is extremely complicated. The political situation has been such that the French Government has not felt willing or able to take a bold stand in respect to this matter. At the beginning of the war the need for airplanes and engines was so great and so urgent that all the European Governments simply accepted practically any terms offered by the manufacturer including very high royalties for the rights to have types of airplanes or engines manufactured elsewhere than in the factories of the owners of such rights. These rights were recognised and the royalties paid by both the home government and by any foreign governments desiring to have these types of airplanes and engines manufactured. I understand that the British Government subsequently commuted many of the royalties paid to its own manufacturers; but the French Government has never felt that it was in a position to do this, although the matter is now under consideration. In Italy the matter is in abeyance and now under consideration. The whole situation is also complicated by the fact that the rights respecting the Hispano Suiza engine emanate from the Spanish Hispano Suiza Company of which I am informed that a majority (said to be four fifths) of the stock is owned by the King of Spain. This seem to have created certain international and diplomatic aspects to the matter which have somewhat embarrassed the French Government. Furthermore the political situation in France seems to have prevented any very determined attitude on the part of the French Government in dealing with its own manufacturers.

When I arrived, I found that the French had constructed the cable from Mr Tardieu [the French High Commissioner to the USA] regarding the $100,000 payments as a firm offer of that amount for each of the airplanes and engines mentioned whether we subsequently decided to build them in America or not. The wording of Mr Tardieu's cable which was shown to be certainly permitted of such construction. Had the French shipped the airplanes and engines immediately, and otherwise carried out their part, the situation might have been embarrassing: but when I returned from Italy, I found that this had not been done. I therefore took a position that $100,000 would be paid only to those manufacturers whose airplanes were adopted for quantity production in the United States. Under our recommendations this would involve only the Spad airplane and the Hispano-Suiza and Gnome Le Rhone engine manufacturers. Both the latter have given some sort of rights to American manufacturers. With respect to these I have taken the position that our rights must emanate directly from the French manufacturers and that they must settle controversies with the American grantees of rights to manufacture these engines. As the engines either will be in America or on their way by the time this report reaches you with full data and engines to assist in the United States production I think this practically settles the matter. As I understand it, these so called rights are not protected by patents, but rest in the power of the manufacturer to disclose or conceal the details of manufacture which make it possible successfully to produce the engines. With the sample engine, full details and assistance of the French engineers it seem that you are in a position to produce these engines independent of American grantees of any so called rights. If those American grantees have any claim against the French manufacturers based upon contract, the French manufacturers will have to deal with that situation themselves as I have told them, I do not see how American grantees can enforce any claim against the United States Government.

However, you will see that it would be inconsistent for us to say to the British and French Governments that you must take care of the situation with respect to their citizens unless we also say that we will take care of the situation with respect to our citizens. In that I do not see any difference between the citizens of the United States who have so called rights by reason of being manufacturers of airplanes and engines and American citizens who have so called rights by reason of licences which they have purchased. We must take care of the situation in America if the foreign governments are to take care of the situation in England and in France.

With respect to any claims for future royalties, I have taken the position that while the matter was left open for subsequent negotiation under your arrangements with Mr Tardieu, and I will listen to anything the French Government or its manufacturers care to say on the subject, I cannot entertain any such claims. The action of the British Government makes it possible to maintain this position. Meanwhile you will be in a position to go ahead and manufacture the airplanes and engines which seems to me to settle the matter. While there may be some further talk, I think this disposes of the French royalty situation.

The Italian Army Officers in charge of their production recognise the justice of the American position with respect to royalties. They now have under advisement their own relations in the matter to their manufacturers. The situation is simplified somewhat by the fact that most of the developments in Italy have been carried out under the Italian Army. They have already dispatched to America everything which we asked and I do not anticipate any difficulty in dealing with the royalty situation, although it may be necessary to make some moderate payment such as will be given to the French. The Capron is the only airplane at present recommended for American production and by the time this report arrives you should have all you need to start its production.

SAMPLES, AIRPLANES, ENGINES, AND DATA NECESSARY FOR THEIR PRODUCTION; I fully appreciate the disappointment which must have followed the delays to get the desired sample airplanes and engines and information covering their manufacture in America, We have felt this disappointment as much as anybody could, but every possible action has been taken by us to expedite the matter here. In England and Italy I think the airplanes, engines etc., were dispatched as promptly as could be expected under the circumstances. In France, the United States requirements had been indicated and agreed to before we arrived and we were told that everything was either already on the way to ship board or being prepared for immediate shipment. It was not until we returned from Italy and Major Tulanne was given charge of the situation that we found that practically nothing had been done. As I have indicted, there has meanwhile occurred one of the frequent changes in the French Government Department in charge of the matter. All I can say is, first, that you can hardly realize the difficulties of apparently simple matters of this sort in countries where every bit of transportation and everything else is part of a complex and cumbersome system of military administration. Second, that the foreign manufacturers have a surprising lack of data covering articles of their manufacture. In most of the airplanes and engines factories are entirely without complete drawings, specifications and other tabulated information which we would consider essential in the manufacture of airplanes and engines. After all, you may well consider in this connection what would happen in the case of similar requests made to our Government.

AMERICAN PRODUCTION PROGRAM; There is general agreement here in the opinion we have formed concerning the governing principle for our American production program. This opinion is as follows:

First, The United States must first provide itself with all airplanes and engines required for training purposes in America.

Second, The United States must next provide the airplanes and engines necessary for use strictly in connection with the operation of American forces in the field. It is best known in Washington what will be the size and composition of the American forces in the field at any given dates in the future. You have information as to the number and types of airplanes required in direct connection with military operations of these forces. We have learned nothing to change the views on that matter which were held by Major Foulois when we left Washington.

Third. After these considerations come the American program of putting into the field next year air forces in excess of the tactical requirements of its Army in France. It is greatly desired that the United States shall do this. Such air forces should consist of fighting airplanes and bombers. The fighting airplanes are divided into two classes;

(a) Airplanes with fixed engines

(b) Airplanes with rotary engines

Both types appear to be essential. We hold the opinion that the rotary engine is much less reliable and has much less length of service than the stationary engine; but for certain purposes it appears to be indispensable. The bombing airplanes may be divided into day and night bombers. Day bombing presents much greater difficulties than night bombing because it cannot be conducted successfully by slow machine of great bomb-carrying capacity, if the enemy have in the air any number of fast fighting machines or have great numbers of anti-aircraft guns effective at great altitudes. If it should be possible to drive from the air practically all the enemy fighting machines, day bombing would become more effective. Night bombing allows to use large aeroplanes without great speeds but with great bomb-carrying capacity. There is practically no effective means of preventing night bombing. Therefore, it possibilities appear to depend almost entirely on the number of suitable airplanes which can be provided. From the military standpoint these possibilities are very great and extremely important. Could night bombing be conducted on a sufficiently great scale and kept up continuously for a sufficient time there seems good reason to believe that it might determine the whole outcome of military operations. Up to the present time, the trouble seems to have been that all bombing has been carried out intermittently and sporadically because of the lack of attention to the subject and provision for large enough numbers of the right kind of airplanes. In this connection, it may be well to compare the situation with artillery bombardment. While I speak with some diffidence on such a subject, all I have been able to learn indicates that intermittent and sporadic artillery bombardment produces but small result notwithstanding the great size and accuracy of modern bombardment artillery. When definite and important results are desired, artillery bombardment must be made systematic and continuous and tremendous quantities of high explosives must be used on the selected objectives. This seems to be exactly the situation which exists in respect to airplane bombardment. There seems every reason to believe that it can be made of vital importance if very great numbers of airplanes carrying great size and numbers of bombs can be provided and used continuously and systematically.

To determine the proportion of airplanes of different types for United States production we have recommended the following rough method of calculation which seems to give results that check up pretty well with the views over here: first, deduct form the total number of airplanes it is considered possible to produce, the total number required for use in direct connection with the military forces. That number can only be determined where it is known what will be the size of the military forces at any given time and that number varies only in proportion to the size of the forces. By this deduction having obtained the number of airplanes within your capacity of production which can be used independently of United States military forces, we recommend this number is proportioned as follows; About thirty seven and a half percent should be fighting airplanes divided equally between fixed and rotary engine fighters. About twenty five percent should be day bombers and about thirty seven and a half percent should be night bombers. Of course it is impossible to establish any proportions that are likely to be entirely correct because it is impossible to tell what will be the air conditions at any given time. For example, the enemy may have a larger or smaller number of fast fighting machines requiring that we have a larger or smaller number of these machines permitting our use of a smaller number of day bombing machines.

TYPES FOR AMERICAN PRODUCTION; Our cables and the reports of Captains Clark and Marmon should furnish a full statement of our conclusions concerning the types of airplanes and engines recommended for quantity production in America. I regard to these recommendations I can only add that the difficulty of deciding upon types of airplanes and engines for different purposes, particularly the difficulty of deciding for production some distances in the future, has been greater then could possibly be realised without visiting England, France and Italy.

We recommend the following airplanes and engines;

Airplanes

Advanced training Bristol Scout with 80hp Le Rhone.

Division or Corps d'Armee Bristol Fighter with 200hp Hispano.

Long Range Reconnaissance and day bombing D.H.4 with Rolls Royce or some other equivalent engine to be later copied. Fiat 300 has proved successful here.

Fighting or Pursuit (fixed engine) Spad with 200hp Hispano.

Fighting or Pursuit (rotary engine) New Spad with 150 Gnome (this airplane is now undergoing final tests)

Night Bombing Caproni Triplane with 3 Isotta Fraschini 270hp engines or equivalent engine to be later adopted. For very long distance bombing with heavy loads the Italians are now arranging to use the Caproni Biplane with 3 Isotta Fraschini engines instead of the heavier Fiats now used. For distances of 400-500 miles (out and back included) the much greater consumption of gasoline and oil by the Triplane gives it little greater bomb carrying capacity then the Biplane with Isotta Fraschini engines and the Biplane can be produced much more quickly and in greater quantities. It is also much easier to house at the front. For bombing at shorter distances nothing gives such great bomb carrying capacity as the Triplane.

Engines

80 hp Le Rhone for training purposes

200 hp Hispano Suiza for fixed engine one place fighters and division or Corps d'Armee airplanes

150 Gnome Monosoupape for rotary engine fighters

Rolls-Royce for U.S. production only under some special arrangement of a Rolls-Royce factory in U.S. This engine is not considered suitable for great quantity production. It also requires very skilled mechanics to keep it in commission at the front.

While we have investigated many other excellent engines such as Renault, Fiat, Isotta-Fraschini and S.P.A. all of them are too heavy per horsepower to be recommended as engines for great quantity future production in the U.S.

Renault, Fiat and Isotta- Fraschini all have new designs under test that might prove very desirable. The Bugatti engine appears perhaps to offer the most interesting future development for light weight per horsepower and ease of quantity production. The developments with our U.S. engine now under test are probably the most important consideration in this question of engine production in the U.S. of course, we are without any adequate information over here as to these developments.

CONCLUSION—The extreme complexity and difficulty of the conditions under which our work has been done and the pressure under which this report must be prepared leads me to ask some indulgence in its consideration. We have tried to do our best under most difficult conditions and no effort in our power has been omitted in the endeavor

> to do our work as well and as quickly as possible. In conclusion, I wish to express the warmest personal appreciation of the work of all the party among whom there has been the greatest harmony and every effort to carry out the common purpose.
> Respectfully submitted, R.C. BOLLING

Bolling, and the other members of the mission had indeed worked with commendable speed and diligence. As a result, some of the selections made for quantity production may have been a little odd, perhaps evidencing the haste with which the selections had needed to be made; for example, the Bristol Scout was out of date, even as a trainer, and the Bristol Fighter would be rather underpowered with only a 200-hp Hispano engine instead of the 275-hp Rolls-Royce with which it was normally fitted. Although the mission was, as Bolling had stated in his conclusion, out of touch with developments back home, at least America now had a much better idea of what aeroplanes it needed to manufacture, and its factories could finally get to work on producing them.

6

# Financing the Plan

Once the Aviation Section had committed itself to meeting as far as was possible the French Premier's proposals, Benjamin Foulois and his fellow officers prepared huge flow charts, written on sheets of wrapping paper obtained from a local store, to calculate how the programme should work. They calculated that the sum of almost $640 million would be needed to fund not just the manufacture of the aeroplanes and their engines, including the cost of those purchased abroad, but the expansion of the Aeronautical Division generally, including creating new airfields and training the crews and mechanics. With all this information before him, Gen. George Squier, Chief Officer of the Signal Corps, made a direct appeal to Secretary of War Newton D. Baker for the funds to be made available to purchase 22,625 aeroplanes and train all the aviators needed to operate them. On 9 July, Gen. Squier appeared before the House of Representatives, hoping to ease the passage of the Bill that would make all this possible.

In addition to the on-going propaganda seeking to ensure that public opinion remained in support of the war, and to recruit for the armed forces, attempts were also made to convince the American people, and thus their political representatives, of the benefits of waging war in the air. However, Gen. Pershing, commander of the American Forces in France, thought that the cost of such publicity would have been better used for more direct military purposes.

The Bill was formally put before the House of Representatives on 11 July, explaining that some $125.29 million would be spent on aeroplanes, $239.85 million on their engines, and $200 million on developing new airfields, on training, and on expendables. Other, smaller sums were included for miscellaneous purposes, with $45 million included for naval aviation, bringing the requirement to a remarkably precise total of

This illustration, published in *Flying* magazine in August 1917, demonstrates America's expectations of its aircraft production programme, and was typical of the many appeals to American patriotism made at that time.

$639,241,658, rounded up to an even $640 million. Details of exactly how many aeroplanes were involved, or which types were intended, were withheld, it was said, in the interests of secrecy.

Despite the enormity of the sum of money involved, which was more than forty times greater than any single budget debated and approved during the previous fiscal year, the House approved the Bill without a division and without dissent after only four hours of debate. The proposal was approved by the Senate, with an equal lack of opposition, in what was described in the press as being 'a spirit of patriotic compliance' on 21 July. It was passed to President Woodrow Wilson for signature, becoming law on 24 July as The Aviation Act (40. Stat. 243), the biggest single appropriation of funds Congress had ever made up to that date.

The money was to be raised, in part—together with the other massive costs of modern war—by the sale of Government securities known almost inevitably as 'Liberty Bonds'. Several billions were raised from each of four successive issues, made throughout the war, each at a slightly higher rate of interest to help persuade the people to keep on investing.

The Aviation Act not only appropriated the funding required to create the aerial armada that the publicity had promised, but also made changes to the way in which the Aviation Section—now increasingly referred to simply as the Air Service—was supported. It authorised the Equipment

One of the many posters and similar advertisements designed to encourage Americans to invest in the cost of the war.

Division to take responsibility for the procurement and distribution of aeronautical supplies; the Construction Division to build and maintain airfields; the Aircraft Engineering Division to conduct research and produce new designs; and the Wood Division to provide adequate supplies of timber, most especially spruce, for aeroplane construction. Although some of these bodies were later renamed, their existence and their function would continue unaltered throughout the war.

The Equipment Division, which would place the orders for the manufacture of aeroplanes and engines, comprised Edward A. Deeds at its head, with R. L. Montgomery and Sidney Waldon from the Aircraft Production Board, together with Jesse Vincent, co-designer of the Liberty engine, and five others—Harold .H. Emmons, Leonard S. Horner, George W. Mixter, Harry L. Shepter, and Melville W. Thompson. All were commissioned into the Army with the exception of Emmons, an attorney, who was already a member of the Navy Reserve.

In England, *Flight* magazine commented favourably, stating that this huge sum of money, which it converted into sterling at the prevailing rate of exchange as £128 million, showed America's commitment to the Allied cause and added that it thought that it should provide a sufficiently large air service to help to win the war.

Germany's views on the matter are unrecorded.

7

# The Orders are Placed

Almost four months had now elapsed since America had entered the war, during which time orders for training machines had been placed in accordance with Howard Coffin's earlier report with Curtiss and Standard, each for their own designs, Dayton-Wright, and the Fisher Body Company, for these same designs.

Founded in 1908, by members of a family that had been making carriages for generations, the Fisher Body Company of Detroit built motor car bodies for a number of automobile manufacturers, including Buick, Cadillac, Ford, and Studebaker. By 1914, it had become the largest company of its kind in the world, and by 1916, it was producing well over 350,000 bodies each year; already familiar with mass production, and with acres of factory floor space, it appeared well suited to aeroplane manufacture.

Dayton-Wright, on the other hand, was a brand-new company, established expressly to profit from making munitions. Following Wilbur Wright's death in 1912, Orville appears to have lost much of his former enthusiasm for aviation; in 1915, he sold the Wright Company, as recorded earlier, to Glen Martin. Wright-Martin moved away from Dayton in March 1917, leaving the former Wright Company building empty.

A group of Dayton-based businessmen, including Edward Deeds, took over the building, together with a number of former employees of the Wright and Wright-Martin companies, and formed Dayton-Wright, the new company being incorporated just days after America's entry into the war. It occupied various premises, including the former Wright factory, where metal fittings were fabricated, and a large plant at Moraine, Ohio, which had been built for the manufacture of generating sets by Delco.

Orville had no shares in the new business, being employed as a 'consultant' largely for the kudos still attached to his name as co-inventor of the aeroplane.

One of the Fisher Body company's factories in Detroit. The world's leading manufacturer of motor car bodies turned to aircraft production in 1917, returning to the motor industry after the war.

The Wright Company's factory buildings in Dayton, Ohio, which were taken over by the Dayton-Wright Company as Plant No. 3. The buildings survive to this day.

On being appointed to the Aircraft Production Board, Deeds transferred his own interest in the company to a third party, but remained associated through other business interests with its new owners.

By mid-1917, 192 separate patents relating to aeronautical matters had been granted in the US, and previous efforts to establish a patent pool had failed, largely because the Wright company, and its successors' (which held the key patent) control in the rolling plan, refused to join. However, on 26 July 1917, a cross licensing agreement was finally made whereby aircraft manufacturers paid a small fee for each machine produced, which was then shared among the patent holders.

Up to this time, each American aeroplane maker had used their own controls systems, partly with a view to circumvent Wright's patents. Yet in late July 1917, the Society of Automotive Engineers, in whose hands aeroplane manufacture was about to be placed, recommended the adoption of not only a standardised control system, employing a control column and rudder bar, but also standardised designs for turnbuckles, thimbles, and for the loop ends of both hard wires and flexible cables, simplifying both maintenance and the stocking of spare parts.

In August 1917, with the funding made available by Congress, and with the Bolling Mission's recommendations made, America was finally in a position to begin production of combat aeroplanes—the key date of 1 July 1918 still eleven months away. Yet the arrival of the sample aeroplanes, and their accompanying drawings and specifications, revealed problems that appear not to have been previously considered. The ship carrying the sample D.H.4, A7531, which had been supplied without either engine of armament, docked in New York on 18 July and the aeroplane was taken first to Washington DC and then on to McCook field at Dayton, Ohio, where it arrived on 15 August. The drawings, although fairly detailed, where all drawn in first angle projection, as was normal European practice, but engineers in America were used to an different system, third angle projection, in which the top, front, and side views of a component are differently arranged. In addition, it was realised that standard gauges, for wire diameters and sheet metal thicknesses, differ between England and the US and that no direct equivalents existed. In England, '10 gauge' steel sheet was 0.125 inches thick, but in America, the '10 gauge' had, and still has, a thickness of 0.134 inches. This meant that many components needed not only to be redrawn, to ensure that American engineers did not misinterpret the drawings, but also restressed as the use of a thinner gauge of metal would obviously reduce the strength of the component, while a thicker gauge would increase its weight, both alternative affecting its overall performance. Bolt sizes and their thread patterns also differed between the two countries and had to be recalculated, all of which took time, delaying the commencement of actual production.

The samples from France and Italy, when they finally arrived, brought a further complication: the metric system of measurement with which American engineers were wholly unfamiliar. Machine tools lacked the scales to be set to metric units and, again, the only solution was to redesign each and every affected part, using a system American factory workers could understand and their machine tools accommodate.

The other sample aeroplanes, requested by the Bolling Mission while in Europe, took slightly longer to arrive with, for example, the Bristol F.2B Fighter reaching New York on 25 August and the SPAD arriving there on 12 September.

It also became necessary to redesign the D.H.4 to accommodate the Liberty engine when, fairly early on, it became apparent that the Rolls-Royce engine that powered the majority of the English versions would not be available. Not only was the engine wholly unsuited to assembly line production in the American way—Col. Bolling having previously commented in a letter that 'there are numbers of firms in the U.S who could manufacture the engine but it is not an easy thing to do as it is more or less a hand made affair'—but the Rolls-Royce company were reluctant to pass technical information and manufacturing secrets on to American companies, like Packard, who would again become their business rivals once the war was over.

Even building the Liberty engine, designed specifically for manufacture by American workers in American factories, encountered delays. Development of the 225-hp eight-cylinder version, which had been the first model built, was discontinued on the advice of Gen. Pershing in France, as aircraft in service there needed engines of higher power. As the four- and six-cylinder versions virtually duplicated the power of other engines that were already in production, they too were not developed further, leaving the L12 as the standard model.

Originally tested in August 1917 at 330 hp, the twelve-cylinder version was quickly developed to deliver 400 hp to meet the constant demand for ever better performance. The oil feed system was redesigned and, following failures due to torsional vibration, which was little understood at the time, the crankshaft was strengthened, reducing, if not entirely eliminating, the problem. Design changes continued to be made even after the engine had been put into production, which is normal for any aero engine, but which created an unwelcome inconvenience both to mass production and to the interchangeability of parts. However, reliability and the time between overhauls were both very similar to those of other comparable engines in service at the time, and caused no serious concerns.

Cylinder manufacture was also a problem until Ford developed a method of making them by cutting and pressing steel tube to produce the closed-end cylinders into which the valves seats were then cut. As a result, the Ford Motor Company took on the manufacture of all of the Liberty engine cylinders made, producing a total of over 433,000, contributing significantly to the company's wartime profits of almost $5 million.

Pricing, both for components and for complete engines, was curiously complex; a unit 'bogey' price was estimated, and contractors were then allowed a set profit on this price, on a cost plus basis, but should efficiency in manufacture, reduction in material costs, or any other cause create a saving on the bogey price, the manufacturer was allowed to retain 25 per cent of this saving in addition to the original agreed profit—the remainder going back to the Government.

Since it had been designed specifically for mass production, contracts to build the Liberty were given only to companies considered large enough to produce it in significant numbers. Therefore, despite Elbert Hall's contribution to its design, the Hall-Scott company received no orders. The first formal order to manufacture the Liberty L12 appears to have been that placed with Nordyke and Marmon, for 3,000 units, on 5 September 1917. This was followed the next day by an order for 500, placed with the Trego Motor Corporation. Packard received an official order for 6,000 engines on 11 October as did the recently formed Lincoln Motor Company, which set up a new factory and bought over 90,000 special tools in order to fulfil the contract. Its founder, Henry M. Leland, had resigned from the Cadillac company, which he had previously founded, as its current owners, General Motors, initially refused to accept armaments contracts. Leland had the new company named after the great President Abraham Lincoln, whom he greatly admired, with the view to converting to automobile manufacturer once the war was over.

The Ford Motor Company received an order for 5,000 complete engines on 31 October, in addition to being contracted to produce the cylinders for every engine ordered from any manufacturer. William C. Durant, President of General Motors, was a pacifist and initially refused to allow production of war material in his factory. He later relented, and on 12 December, the Buick Company, which was under his control, accepted an order to build the Liberty. A total of 3,000 of the completed engines were to be shipped to Britain, for use in her own aircraft production.

The iron, steel, and aluminium needed for the manufacture of aero engines was easily obtainable, and no shortages ever occurred, but the diverse range of materials needed for the construction of aeroplanes was less readily available.

The majority of the wood used in aeroplane construction was spruce, which is strong for its weight, straight grained, and easy to work. The major source of supply was in the forests of America's North West, where the trees grew up to 200 feet tall. America had been supplying spruce to Europe as a normal commercial enterprise long before its entry into the war. With the formulation of America's own aircraft building programme, supplies to Europe were restricted, preserving the vital material for America's own use and alternative timber, much of it Cypress, substituted. Widely used for construction work in America's southern states where it was grown, on paper this appeared acceptable for lightly stressed components and in training machines, where an extra weight could be accommodated. In practice, it prove unsuitable, and the British Government was eventually obliged to discontinue its use, buying back all stocks held by aeroplane manufacturing companies at cost, plus a small percentage handing charge.

However, even by carefully husbanding supplies for America's own use, the normal commercial logging operations in Oregon and Washington State proved unable to keep pace with demand and eventually the Army stepped in. New roads and railways were laid, the former to provide access into the forests and the latter to transport the cut timber away, and mills were built to saw the huge logs. Some 50,000 troops, all on the roster of the Signal Corps, joined the civilian lumbermen, whose wages and working conditions were, of necessity, improved, ending discontent among them. Once initial problems, especially with kiln drying, were overcome, the quantity of timber producing improved dramatically, ending shortages of this vital material. In November 1918, after the Armistice, Brig.-Gen. Brice P. Disque, the officer commanding the Spruce Production Division, sent his officers and men the following message:

> The Great War is over and for the world, for the nation, and for ourselves we are thankful. Our part has been carried on far from the battle front with no chance for distinguished service in combat but let every man remember always that without the airplane lumber which we, practically alone, have furnished for the entire allied cause, this day of thanksgiving could not have been.
>
> You, as well as your comrades overseas, have won this war and a feeling of duty well done should prevail in your hearts this day and every day throughout the great future that lies before each of you.
>
> I congratulate you upon your achievement, and from the bottom of my heart I thank you.

Linen, with which aeroplanes were then usually covered, is made from the fibres of the flax plant, from which linseed oil is also obtained. Its manufacture is labour intensive, making it relatively expensive when compared to other cloth, but it is more than twice as strong as a comparable weight cotton. The most famous, and arguably the best, source for linen is Ireland, although it is produced all over the world, wherever the flax plant

Forestry workers posing with a newly felled spruce log in America's North West. Around 50,000 troops assisted the forestry workers to meet the demand for spruce for aircraft production.

Soldiers of the spruce division pose for a photograph. Their contribution to America's war effort was rightly considered just as important as that of combat troops in France can be grown. It does grow in America, in areas around Wisconsin, but the demand to meet America's sudden and dramatic increase in aeroplane manufacture soon outpaced supply, and in August 1917, the US Bureau of Standards agreed a specification for the substitution, where necessary, of Grade A cotton fabric, the raw material for which was grown, in great abundance, in America's southern states.

Over 100,000 acres of farmland in the warmer regions of the US were given over to growing the tropic plant *Ricinus Communis*, a flowering shrub from the seeds of which castor oil is obtained, in order to ensure an adequate supply of lubricating oil of the type then most favoured for aeroplane engines. All the numerous other materials, including wire, ferrules, and turnbuckles, paint, dope and varnish, and a wide variety of other diverse materials needed to construct an aeroplane of the era, America was easily about to supply from her own vast resources, building new factories whenever necessary.

Volume orders for training machines were placed late in June, funded by the initial appropriations, with Curtiss receiving an order for 600 JN-4 trainers on 30 June. This was followed, after a more extensive expansion of the Air Service had been approved, by a further order of 1,400 JN-4s in September. All these aircraft were duly manufactured. However, a contract placed with the Standard Aircraft Corporation for 250 examples of its SJ-1 Trainer on 23 July 1917 was reduced to 100 on 4 October after the first forty-four machines had been delivered, but then a further 500 machines were ordered on the same day. All 600 were completed.

Contracts awarded to other companies appear to have been even equally indecisive; Dayton-Wright was awarded a contract for 500 JN-4s on 21 June, in accordance with Coffin's proposal that the company should begin with building training aircraft before changing to front-line types, only to have this replaced by an order for 400 SJ-1s on 28 July, probably because the engines for the JN-4s could not be made available. Fisher Body was also affected by this indecision, receiving similar orders and then similar amendments to those orders. However, both companies satisfactorily completed the finalised contracts, each building 400 of the training machines so vital to the expansion of the Air Service.

Contracts to build front-line types were subject to even more amendments, both to accommodate administrative changes and to keep abreast of developments at the front. Orders were cancelled and reissued often for the same number and type of aircraft, with new batches of serial numbers included in each new order. Often, this was done when something changed—the agreed price or the type of engine to be fitted—but on occasion, no reason for the change was apparent.

Another administrative change, made as America strove to refine its procedures, came into effect on 1 October 1917 when all duties of

Building aeroplane wings at the Fisher Body factory. The work proved to be more delicate and more demanding than producing motor car bodies, and the workforce took some time to adapt.

the Aircraft Production Board were transferred to the newly created Aircraft Board, which retained the same members, along with additional representatives of the Army and Navy. However, while still an advisory body, it now had statutory authority, and was made responsible to the Secretaries of the Army and Navy instead of to the Council of National Defence.

Further changes were made in May 1918, when the Air Service was made a separate branch of the US Army, no longer part of the Signal Corps. Two new bodies, the Department of Military Aeronautics and the Bureau of Aircraft Production (headed by Mr John D. Ryan), were created at the same time, each directly responsible to the Secretary of War. This furthered the duality of control that already existed, but rendered the Aircraft Board, from which Howard Coffin had already resigned, virtually obsolete, forcing it to fade into obscurity.

Within weeks of the completion of Bolling's Mission, developments in Europe also began to necessitate change to its proposals, especially if America was to maintain its commitment to providing an aerial fleet of the latest types. As a result, the proposed programme was revised, as indeed it had previously been on several occasions, and would be again in the future.

The new rotary engined SPAD fighter proved a failure at its official trials, and as it was not adopted for production in France, it was dropped from America's programme. The Sopwith was also dropped due to problems with producing the rotary engine, which powered it, in American factories. In England, there were proposals for the D.H.4 to be superseded by the D.H.9, which had a different engine and in which the two cockpits were closer together, improving crew communication and so eliminating the most notable flaw in the D.H.4's design; America considered following suit, and began to amend its proposal before reverting to the earlier design when the D.H.9 proved a disappointment after first entering service. The Caproni triplane had lost favour, the biplane version now being preferred, although the Handley Page O/400 bomber was now also being considered as an alternative.

On 4 October 1917, a letter from E. S. Gorrell brought the news that the 200-hp geared Hispano-Suiza, which was to power the SPAD and Bristol Fighter, was proving unreliable and alternative engines needed to be sought. The problem turned out to be largely due to imperfectly hardened gears, but in England, several hundred newly built aeroplanes, which were badly needed in action, were stockpiled awaiting their engines before the problem was finally resolved.

The Martinsyde F3, an advanced new fighter, powered by the Rolls-Royce 'Falcon' engine, made its first flight at Brooklands in September 1917, its performance so impressive that it was hoped that it would replace existing in-line engined fighters in France. On 8 October, a block order for 500, along with other types, was placed with Dayton-Wright. However, this was soon cancelled due to changes in the types required, and when reissued, the Martinsyde was no longer included, probably as a result of policy changes, and none were built in the USA.

Although fighter aircraft were initially included in the programme, it seems that the performance and combat capability of two seaters such as the Bristol F.2B appeared to the US headquarters in Europe to highlight a future trend. On 8 November 1917, cable No. 252, sent from Europe over Bolling's name, stated: 'Single Seat fighter will probably be obsolete [for] general use next year, although small numbers will always be used [for] special purposes'.

This opinion was reinforced a few weeks later in cable 375, in which Gen. Pershing recommended leaving fighter production to companies in Europe.

It therefore decided that only examples of single-seat fighters already in production should be completed, those already being purchased in France presumably being considered sufficient to fulfil both immediate needs and any requirements for 'special purposes'.

With all these changes happening, it was inevitable that some of the other types of aircraft included either in the Aircraft Production Board's preliminary proposal, or recommended by the Bolling Mission, were never ordered, or were cancelled, often with another type being substituted. For both simplicity and completeness, we shall now look at each major design individually.

8

# Curtiss JN-4

The JN series of two-seat aircraft were initially designed by Benjamin D. Thomas, formerly of the Sopwith Aviation Company in England, who moved to America to join Curtiss and combined features of both the earlier J type, built for the US Army, and the Navy's N type. The JN-1 and JN-2 variants, of which only a few were built, employed the shoulder yoke aileron control previously used in Curtiss pushers, but the JN-3 had its lateral control operated by a wheel. Examples saw active service with the Signal Corps during the Mexico campaign, and were bought as trainers for the RFC in Britain.

A further improved version, the JN-4, replaced the wheel with a more conventional control column, its construction was equally conventional and it was stable and relatively easy to fly, making it ideal for initial pilot training. Like the earlier versions, it was powered by the 90-hp water-cooled OX-5 engine designed by Curtiss and built in the factory at Hammondsport. It was well established by the time of America's entry into the war, with a number of small orders for the US Signal Corps, and for both the RFC and RNAS in England, already completed.

The Aircraft Production Board's initial proposals, dated 13 June 1917, called for the building of 5,000 JN-4s and noted: 'This program is already under way'. If so, negotiations must still have been at a preliminary stage as the first formal orders do not appear to have been placed until a little later, with both Fisher Body and Dayton-Wright receiving orders, each for 500 aircraft, on 21 June. It was proposed that these should be powered by the Hall-Scott A7 engine, but these orders were subsequently cancelled and replaced with orders for the Standard J-1, which was normally powered by that engine.

The Curtiss Company received an order for 600 JN-4s on 30 June 1917, followed by a further order for 1,400 on 15 September, all of which were completed and delivered on time.

Orders were also placed with a number of other, smaller companies, several of which, including an order for 300 placed with Liberty Iron on 28 September, and an order for 100 given to US Aircraft on 13 October, were later reduced in number due to late deliveries, although the balance of the US Aircraft batch was later reordered.

At least six companies, as well as Curtiss, eventually manufactured the JN-4, a total of 6,813 being completed with at least 95 per cent of all pilots trained in America having flown one.

The JN-4H variant, powered by the 150-hp Hispano-Suiza engine, was introduced as an advanced trainer to bridge the gap between the OX-5-powered JN-4D and service types, with 929 being completed all by Curtiss.

After the war, surplus 'Jennies', as the type had become known, were sold off cheaply, and formed the backbone of civil aviation in America during the 1920s. It also remained in service with the US Air Service as a trainer until 1927, and the Curtiss Company continued to manufacture spare parts until that year.

Approximately fifty examples remain extant today, in museums and in private ownership.

9

# Standard J-1

Similar to the Curtiss JN-4 both in appearance and performance, the Standard J-1 was designed by Charles H. Day of the Standard Aircraft Corporation, Plainsfield, New Jersey. It made its first flight in 1916, the same year that the company was incorporated. In October, an order for eighteen machines was placed by the Signal Corps, the machines being intended from the outset for training purposes. Power was provided by the four-cylinder inline water-cooled Hall Scott A7 engine.

Orders placed with Standard (250) and Dayton-Wright and Fisher Body (400 each) on 28 July 1917, replaced the cancelled orders for the Curtiss JN-4. The order with Standard was later renegotiated, with a revised price and new serials allotted, before completion of the contract.

Although the J-1 was not as well liked as the JN-4, being considered more difficult to fly and vibrating badly under certain conditions, further orders were placed with all three companies and with Wright-Martin. The new orders with Dayton-Wright were later cancelled so that production facilities could be concentrated on the D.H.4, but a total of 1,601 were completed before, in June 1918, the design was grounded as the engine was considered too unreliable, often catching fire in the air. Although conversion to the Curtiss OX-5 was considered, the cost appeared prohibitive and it seemed sensible to concentrate on production of the more popular Curtiss JN-4.

The Standard was relegated to use as a ground instructional airframe, with many being sold off to civilian operators, often still in their delivery crates, and orders for a further 2,600 were cancelled.

Fitted with alternative engines, most often either the OX-5 or Hispano-Suiza, the J-1 continued in private ownership after the war, although in smaller numbers than the more popular Curtiss design, with a few remaining extant, largely in museums, to this day.

Standard J-1 trainers lined up at Call Field, Texas, in 1918. The type was never as popular as the more numerous Curtiss JN-4 largely due to problems with its engine .

# 10

# Bristol Scout D

Designed by Frank Barnwell at the British and Colonial Aircraft Company, the Bristol Scout first flew early in 1914 and, with the coming of war, was quickly adopted for military use. It developed through four models, A–D, each a slight improvement on the previous version. A total of around 375 were built, with the model D built in the greatest numbers. The Scout served with both the RFC and RNAS in almost every theatre of the war around the world. Its initial wartime role was as a fighter before being relegated, as many out-dated aircraft were, to a training role. It was easy and pleasant to fly, being entirely without vices, and its popularity with pilots led to it being recommended to the Bolling Mission as an advanced trainer to bridge the gap between such machines as the Curtiss JN-4 and front-line types such as the SPAD. Thus, on 28 June, two days after his arrival in England, Bolling sent a cable recording his progress and stating that he had arranged for a sample Bristol Scout and an 80-hp Le Rhône engine to power it. The engine was shipped on 28 July, and on arrival, it taken to Washington, with the aeroplane, B763, following about two weeks later. On 9 August, just as B763 was leaving England, a revised production programme included plans to build 750 Bristol Scouts, and a meeting of the Aircraft Production Board a month later recommended increasing this number to 900, suggesting that the contract be given to the Fisher Body Company.

B763 had been built at No. 1 (Southern) Aircraft Repair Depot at Farnborough and was largely assembled from spare parts—such rebuilt aeroplanes was fairly commonplace in RFC service. It was sent to the Thomas Morse Aircraft Corporation at Ithaca, New York, for drawings to be prepared, redesigning it to facilitate manufacture in America, an operation that presumably required it to be dismantled.

It appears to have remained there until the following spring, arriving at McCook Field in Dayton on 25 April 1918 in poor condition and with some components missing.

Thomas Morse's own rival model, the S.4, designed by Benjamin Thomas (no relation) who had previously worked at both Sopwith and at Curtiss where he had designed the first of the JN series of trainers, had made its first flight in June 1917, flown from the field at Ithaca by company test pilot Frank Burnside. It was then sent to the Army Experimental Flight Station at Hampton, Virginia, where, although its performance was judged satisfactory, details of its construction were criticised. It was also found to be tail heavy in flight. Thomas Morse responded immediately to these official criticisms, stating that the design was being modified to strengthen the components noted as being weak, including the tail skid and wing trailing edges, and to include the other modifications, such as a bigger windscreen, commented on by the Army. An order for fifty (serials 2455–2404) was therefore placed on 11 September, with a further fifty (3926–3975 being added on 25 September. However, as was common throughout the wartime programme, both orders were cancelled on 5 October, a new order, still for 100 machines but of the revised S.4B model, was issued on the same day, together with a new block of serial numbers (4278–4375).

With the Thomas Morse in production, it was logical that it should be included in the next revised production programme, dated 5 November. At the same time, the proposed number of Bristol Scouts was reduced to 500.

No orders had yet been placed manufacture of the Bristol Scout in America and now substitution of the American-designed Thomas Morse as an advanced trainer appeared logical, not out of any spirit of patriotism but because it was thus already suited to mass production in America, free of any need to be redesigned as the Bristol was.

A further revised model, S.4C, which had modified ailerons (improving lateral control), with an operating system based upon that use in Nieuport scouts, and further orders were placed for this model at a price of $5,400 each. The first batch of fifty, ordered on 1 January 1918, were fitted with a 100-hp Gnome engine similar to that in previous models, but for further orders, the 80-hp Le Rhône engine, manufactured by the Union Switch and Signal Company of Swissvale, Pennsylvania, was substituted as this engine was considered more reliable.

While in service, some initial problems with the Thomas Morse became apparent and plans to revive the Bristol Scout were considered. B763 was therefore restored to serve as a pattern, and replacements for the missing components were made in the workshops at McCook field.

The Thomas Morse SV.4C was built as an advanced trainer instead of the Bristol Scout originally considered for the role and proved popular with pilots.

The initial test flight proved difficult and could easily have ended in disaster as the wing struts turned out to be the wrong size, affecting the trim, but it flew satisfactorily once these were replaced with the correct size. In the meantime, however, the problems with the Thomas Morse had been corrected and it continued in service, with plans to build the Bristol again dropped.

A total of 461 Thomas Morse Scouts were completed, a further 553 being cancelled after the Armistice, and the type served with almost every flying training school in the US, proving popular with pilots. Over sixty joined the civil register after the war.

No order was ever placed for the Bristol Scout, and although B763 continued to be flown occasionally at McCook field, its eventual fate is unknown.

11

# Royal Aircraft Factory S.E.5a

Designed at the Royal Aircraft Factory in Farnborough by a team led by Henry Folland, specifically to take advantage of the benefits of the innovative V8 Hispano-Suiza engine, the S.E.5 was designed to be manoeuvrable and yet stable, and easy to fly. The prototype first flew in 1916 and showed remarkable promise, but early in 1917, one crashed due to structural failure of the upper wing, killing the test pilot Frank Goodden. As a result, the wing design had to be modified. A newer version, the S.E.5a, with a revised wing tip profile, further improving the structural strength of the wing, was then introduced, immediately superseding the earlier model, few of which were produced. Over 5,000 were eventually built, equipping many RFC and RAF squadrons throughout the remainder of the war.

Although included in the Aircraft Production Board's preliminary proposals as an advanced trainer, the S.E.5a, which was just coming into service at the time of the Bolling Mission's visit to Europe, was not included in their recommendations—most probably due to fears that it would be superseded by the time that American-built examples could be got to France. In this presumption, Bolling was both right and wrong: the S.E.5a was indeed superseded, but only by improved and more powerful versions of the same design. Therefore, in February 1918, when the single-seat fighter programme was again re-examined, consideration was given to the adoption of the S.E.5a, which was thought easier to fly than the SPAD, as well as being more manoeuvrable and faster in a dive. Four examples, C1115 and C1119–21, all from a batch built by the Royal Aircraft Factory, were shipped to Washington DC to be evaluated for production in the US. On 22 April, the Joint Army and Navy Technical Board recommended that the S.E.5a should be built in America, suggesting the next day that an order be placed for 1,000 machines. A sample machine was therefore shipped to the Curtiss Factory, arriving on 8 May, although, almost inevitably, the accompanying drawings were not considered sufficient to begin production. Once this problem was resolved, the official order for 1,000 machines was formally placed on 8 June 1918, and the serial numbers 43153–44152 assigned. These were to be fitted with 180-hp direct drive Hispano-Suiza engines manufactured in America by Wright-Martin.

Meanwhile, the British Government offered to supply 200 S.E.5as to American squadrons in France, the AEF considering that the SPAD and S.E.5a were the two best fighters available. These were eventually provided from a batch built by the Austin Motor Company, serving with American Squadrons training in England as well as those operating in France. The 141st Aero Squadron commenced operating the S.E.5a in France in October 1918, being joined on 1 November by the 25th Aero Squadron, although the latter was only able to fly two patrols, without encountering any enemy aircraft, before the Armistice came into effect.

A total of 100 S.E.5as, including B503, D340–43, D6079, D6090, D6101–12, and E3905 (all built by Vickers Ltd), together with C8738–57 and C9073–90 (built by Austin), were crated and shipped to America, at least fifty-six being assembled by Curtiss. Almost all retained their British finish and serial numbers except C8740, which became 94078 and was marked P52 at McCook Field, and C9081, which became 94094. Most served with training units, many of them at Kelly Field in Texas, although F8148 is known to have been at Selfridge Field, Michigan.

The first US-built example completed, serial number AS43153, began test flying on 20 August, but was plagued with overheating problems, the summer temperatures in the US being rather higher than those common in Britain, where the machine was designed. The radiator installation, like that of British-built S.E.5as powered by the Wolseley Viper engine, comprised two individual radiator blocks, one either side of the propeller shaft, and so an attempt was made to improve cooling by the provision of a third, smaller block mounted above the shaft between the two existing blocks. This reduced, but did not entirely eliminate, the overheating problem and official tests at Wilbur Wright Field in Dayton were not completed until 2 October, when approval was finally given for production to begin. However, the Armistice took effect before any further examples could be completed and the contract was therefore cancelled, the remainder of the S.E.5as in service in Europe being shipped back to the US for further use there.

An inventory taken on 1 November 1919 showed a total of 204 S.E.5as in service with the US Air Service. Most retained the numerals of

S.E.5a C9087, built by Austin Motors, was one of a batch shipped to America. Although the spacer blocks to which they would have been attached remain fixed to the upper wing, neither the Lewis gun nor its Foster mount are present.

S.E.5a F8006 apparently about to take-off on a patrol. Its markings are those of the 25th Pursuit Squadron, USAS.

their original English serials, with the prefix 'AS' replacing the original initial letter.

Fifty were rebuilt by the Eberhart Steel Products Company of Buffalo, New York, which had been formed in 1918 to manufacture aircraft parts. These were fitted with 180-hp Wright Hispano E engines, and were designated the S.E.5E, receiving the block of serials 22-276 to 22-325, the '22' prefix denoting the fiscal year in which the contract for their manufacture was placed. They differed from the original design in having plywood-covered fuselages and were used, as originally recommended by Howard Coffin's Aircraft Production Board, for advanced training.

By 1926, a total of twenty-six S.E.5s remained in operation with the Air Service, the number dropping to just four by the end of June the following year, although a few had been sold into private ownership, with Air Service's the last survivor, 22-325, ending its service career on 18 January 1929.

An S.E.5 as rebuilt by the Eberhart Steel Corporation flying in America sometime after the war. As was fairly common, the upper engine cowling has been removed to aid engine cooling.

12

# SPAD S.VII and S.XIII

Like the S.E.5, the SPAD S.VII was a single-seat fighter designed around the V8 Hispano-Suiza engine, the prototype making its first flight in May 1916. It was immediately adopted for production, the first examples being delivered in the autumn of the same year. It was a neat, compact, sturdy looking biplane, its wings having no dihedral and, although rigged in a single bay, were fitted with an additional pair of struts each side at the point where the bracing wires crossed. Its wings and tail surfaces each had wire-trailing edges, giving a distinctive scalloped effect. It saw front-line service with both the French and British air services, manufacture also being undertaken in both countries.

A slightly larger, and more powerful version, the S.XIII, fitted with the 200-hp geared version of the Hispano engine, and with twin machine guns, was designed late in 1916 and eventually replaced the earlier version in service. A total of well over 8,000 were built, making it the most numerous type used in the war, with orders for many thousands more being cancelled after the Armistice.

The SPAD was included in both the preliminary proposals made by the Aircraft Production Board as an advanced trainer, and in the recommendations made by the Bolling Mission, as a combat aircraft to be built in the US. The sample SPAD, ordered by Bolling while in France, finally arrived in the US on 12 September 1917, and by 25 September, it had been delivered to the Curtiss factory at Buffalo, New York, so that drawings could be produced, incorporating American measurements to facilitate manufacture in the US. An order for 3,000 machines (serials 5376–8375) was placed with Curtiss on 8 October 1917, but it was soon cancelled; a new order for only 1,500, with new serial numbers, was then substituted. These were presumably intended to be employed as advanced trainers powered by

The SPAD S.VII looked compact and sturdy. This example, serial B9913, was built in England by Mann, Egerton & Co. and was among a small batch exported to America. Many more were purchased in France for service with the USAC.

the 150-hp direct drive Hispano-Suiza engine then being built by Wright-Martin, the cable from Europe, dated 4 October having placed great doubts of the reliability of the 200-hp geared engine. For this order, which included other aircraft types, a third block of serial numbers, 25809–29058, was allocated, but it too was then cancelled on 26 November—probably as a result of the pronouncement in paragraph two of cable No. 375 sent from Gen. Pershing in France on 14 December; this stated that single-seat fighter production was best left to companies in Europe. No formal order was ever issued and the contract therefore became void.

A few examples, imported from France, were assigned Air Service serials. These included two S.VIIs, 94075 and 94099, and two S.XIIIs, 94074 and 94101. A small number of British-built S.VIIs were also shipped to the US. However, no SPAD was ever built in America and plans to build a revised version, powered by the 225-hp eight-cylinder Liberty, were abandoned.

Before his departure from France, Bolling had negotiated the purchase of the aircraft for immediate service directly from the French and, in accordance with Pershing's recommendations, 197 SPAD S.VIIs, complete with engines to power them and all necessary spares, were purchased in December 1917.

One of more than 400 SPAD S.XIIIs that were shipped to the US after the war. The type continued in service there until the 1920s

During 1918, a total of 893 SPAD S.XIIIs were purchased, with fifteen of sixteen squadrons of the AEF in France being equipped with the type by the end of the war. A total of 435 were shipped back to America and some were re-equipped with the lower-powered direct-drive version of the Hispano-Suiza engine, built in America. The type still remained in service into the early 1920s.

Flown, at some point in their career, by most, if not all of America's 'aces', America's most enduring image of a First World War fighter plane is that of the SPAD S.XIII.

13

# Curtiss R-4 and R-6

Recommended in the Aircraft Production Board's preliminary proposal as a reconnaissance machine, the first of the Curtiss R series appeared during 1915 as a large, but entirely conventional two-seat tractor design, rather like an enlargement of the JN design, except that its rudder had a balance area projecting forward over the rather squat fin. As was not uncommon at the time of its design, the pilot occupied the rear cockpit, with the observer in front.

Developed from the improved R-2 of 1915, the R-4 was powered by the 200-hp Curtiss V-2-3 engine, and three were ordered by the US Army before America's entry into the war, some taking part in the Mexico campaign. One hundred were also supplied to Britain for use by the RNAS, its endurance of over six hours making it suitable for over-water patrols. At least two further examples were supplied to the US Army after America entered the war, but further army orders were cancelled to allow preference to the Navy, whose anti-submarine patrols were considered vital to the war effort.

The V-2-3 was reliable, but had a poor power to weight ratio of almost 4 lb per hp, and many of the R-4s in service in America were later being converted to the Liberty engine, which offered almost twice the power for a relatively small increase in weight. At least a further twelve were built, as the R-4L, with the Liberty installed from the start.

The R-6 was similar to the R-4, and was also initially powered by the V-2-3 engine, but was fitted with the longer span, three-bay wings first introduced on the R-3. Seventy-five examples were ordered, mostly as floatplanes, by the US Navy with further small orders placed on behalf of the Army. At least forty of these were also converted to the Liberty engine, as the R-6L, a further 122 of that variant eventually being constructed.

A Curtiss R4L, powered by the Liberty engine, photographed in April 1918.

None of those operated by the American forces saw action during the war.

Post-war, the Navy's R-6s took part in torpedo dropping trials, with some success, while a mail plane version of the R-4 was also developed but saw no service.

14

# Bristol F.2B Fighter

Designed, like the Scout, by the British and Colonial Aeroplane Company's Frank Barnwell, the Bristol Fighter was an attempt to create a two-seater that was better able to defend itself than existing designs. The prototype first flew in the autumn of 1916, powered by an early version of the Rolls-Royce Falcon engine, and immediately made a favourable impression, with production orders being quickly placed. Although its entry into service was undistinguished, with four aircraft being lost on its first patrol, it proved a great success once crews learned how to handle it—not flying it like a normal two seater, relying on the rear gun for defence, but aggressively, attacking with the pilot's gun and with the observer to add a 'sting in its tail'. Being superior in almost every respect to all other two seaters then in service, the RFC planned to re-equip as many of its corps squadrons as possible with the type, and it is therefore hardly surprising that it should have been recommended to the Bolling Mission for adoption by America.

A sample machine, A7207, ordered by Bolling, left England on 15 August, reaching New York on 25 August. On 7 September, it arrived in Washington DC, where it was taken to the Aircraft Exhibition Building, a temporary hangar at the rear of the Smithsonian Institute building.

Bolling had recommended that America should fit the Bristol with the 200-hp Hispano-Suiza engine, as was being tried in England, *in lieu* of the Rolls-Royce Falcon with which the type was usually powered; this latter engine, being a Rolls-Royce design, was not suited to production in America. However, with the reliability of the geared Hispano now in question, plans were quickly made to adapt the design to accommodate the twelve-cylinder Liberty, with Virginius E. Clark, promoted to colonel since his recent return from Europe, being placed in charge of producing the necessary drawings and modifying the forward fuselage to mount both the

*Above:* A British-built Bristol Fighter at a training unit in the UK. The aircraft behind the port wing tip is an Avro 504, Britain's foremost primary trainer. The Bristols were in great demand in France and few found their way to training units.

*Below:* USAO-1s under construction at the Curtiss factory in Buffalo in July 1918, shortly before the contract was cancelled. The Union Flag is hung alongside the Stars and Stripes in honour of the design's British origins.

Liberty Engine and the Marlin machine gun. Thus modified, the machine was officially designated the USAO-1, the 'O' standing for observation, but in practice, it was seldom referred to as anything but a Bristol Fighter.

On 3 November, an order was placed with the Curtiss Company for the construction of 1,000 machines, the sample aeroplane being taken to their Elmwood Plant in Buffalo so that the firm could produce the additional drawings, detailing individual components, required to aid production. By 25 November, sufficient drawings were available for the factory to start work, and on this day, the original order was cancelled and a new order, with a new block of serial numbers issued—presumably because the production of the drawings had revealed some cause to revise the original contract price. This order was, in turn, cancelled and replaced with a new order for 2,000 machines, with the serial numbers 34232–35231, all to be completed by August 1918.

The first machine was completed by 25 January 1918, but it did not make its first flight until 5 March due problems with the engine installation. This led to concerns over the factors of safety included in the drawings produced by the Signal Corps team, and then carried over into those prepared by Curtiss.

By the end of March, the engine problems had been resolved, although revisions to the design, to increase the factor of safety, carried out at the direction of Maj. J. E. Hall, the officer of the Signal Corps' Equipment Division overseeing the project, had rendered many hundreds of the Curtiss factory's detail drawings obsolete. These modifications added yet more weight to that already added by the substitution of the twelve-cylinder Liberty for the original Rolls-Royce engine and by the provision of additional armament, with twin guns firing forward and twin Lewis guns for the observer. Hall would have liked to include even more armament and drew plans for the installation of four forward-firing Marlin guns, but this amendment was fortunately never adopted. He justified the amendments he had made to Clark's design in a letter to the Director of Production, claiming that the design had needed 're-designing and strengthening all the way thru'.

The second machine, incorporating all these amendments, was completed in April, and production to the modified design began in May, with the Army in France still expecting to receive its first squadron equipped with the type. Four more followed in June, nine in July, and more thereafter, with a total of fifty squadrons equipped with the type.

On 5 May, two production examples were delivered to Wilbur Wright Field in Dayton for testing, but two days later, one was lost while being flown by Lt James Doolittle; he had only recently qualified as a pilot, but he later gained fame both as the Winner of the 1925 Schneider Trophy race and leader of the daring Tokyo raid of 1942. As part of a test, Doolittle performed a series of loops, but at the top of the third loop, the fabric peeled of the upper port wing and the machine crashed, landing on some telegraph wires. Both Doolittle and his passenger, Lt W. M. Oler, were unhurt.

A second crash occurred in the afternoon of 10 June, while Lt P. Radar and Lt R. Conner were carrying out a test over the Curtiss field. The fabric peeled away from the upper wing and the machine dived to the ground from around 500 feet, and the petrol tank ruptured and then exploded on impact. Then, on 15 July, Lt Sharp lost control and crashed while performing a barrel role in another USA0-1. Sharp was killed and his passenger, Lt Hale, injured.

Production was halted, and on 20 July, the contract placed with Curtiss was cancelled. Only twenty-seven examples had been completed, but many hundreds more were under construction and had to be scrapped. The total cost of the programme to build the USA0-1, including payments for work carried out and cancellation charges, amounted to $6,482,000.

Defending his original design, Col. Clark wrote to the Director of Military Aeronautics on 12 August 1918:

> I was assigned the task of redesigning the Bristol fighter for the Liberty engine. I was given six weeks working time, very poor facilities, and practically no experienced draftsman with which to do the job. At the end of this time, November 1917, I turned over some 880 drawings made in my department for the new design to the Curtiss Airplane Company. Since that date I have never been called upon to visit the Curtiss factory, nor have I been consulted in any way regarding questions connected with the design or construction....
>
> I designed it to be an observation machine weighing, fully loaded with all necessary equipment, 2940 lbs. There was built a machine which weighed some 700 or 800 lbs more, with changes throughout. The machine that was flown was not the machine designed.

However, the cancellation of the Curtiss contract was not the end of plans to build the Bristol Fighter in America; in June 1918, the original sample machine A7207, now renumbered as P30, was fitted with a 300-hp Hispano-Suiza engine, while a second British-built example, P37, was fitted with an eight-cylinder Liberty, both engines being much closer in power output and weight to those fitted to machines manufactured in England.

P37 crashed before trials could be completed, but P30 showed some promise. The Engineering Division at McCook Field fitted four of the American-built USAO-1 machine with 300-hp Hispano engines,

*Above:* P37, a Bristol Fighter powered by an eight-cylinder Liberty engine. It crashed before testing could be completed.

*Below:* An XB-1A serving with the 13th Aero Squadron post-war.

redesignating them as the USB-1. Following testing, a contract was placed with Curtiss on 1 November 1918 for the manufacture of 2,000 USB-1s, but it was cancelled a few weeks later, following the cessation of hostilities.

On 18 November 1918, P30 gained an unofficial altitude record when it climbed to 29,800 feet over Dayton, Ohio.

Plans to fit four more with the Liberty 8 appear to have been abandoned before completion, but further machines, with ply covered semi-monococque fuselages, were designed and built at McCook Field. These were designated the USXB-1 and USXB-2, the former with twin Marlin machine guns and the latter with Brownings.

Testing took place in July 1919, and the version fitted with Browning machine guns was put into limited production as the XB-1A, a contract for forty being placed with the Dayton-Wright Company on 28 June 1919. This was followed by a further contract for fifty, placed on 25 April 1920. Both contracts were fulfilled and the type served as a night observation aircraft during the 1920s.

15

# Caproni Bombers

The first aircraft designed by Gianni Caproni flew in 1914, and by 1916, his company had developed the Ca.3 bomber (although other designations were also applied to the same model, largely depending upon the type of engines fitted). It was a large three-engined biplane with twin booms and a central nacelle housing a crew of four, two pilots and two gunners, and eventually equipped fifteen bomber squadrons of the *Regia Aeronautica*. It was usually powered by three Isotta Fraschini engines of 150 hp each and often referred to, especially at the Caproni factory, as the Caproni 450. A more powerful development, the Ca.5, with three 200-hp engines was thus designated the Caproni 600.

The much larger Ca.4 was a triplane of the very similar configuration, which made its first flight in 1917 and appears to have greatly impressed the Bolling Mission—it was included in their list of recommended designs for manufacture in America. However, only around fifty examples were ever built by the Caproni company for use in Europe.

A sample Caproni biplane was shipped from Genoa on 1 August 1917, arriving at New York two weeks later, while a Ca.4 triplane left Genoa on 16 August. Each shipment included other sample aeroplanes that Bolling had not requested, but which the Italian authorities hoped the America might buy. On arrival, the Capronis were taken to Langley Field, Virginia, for assembly and testing, all carried out by the Italian personnel that had accompanied them. The Americans were merely allowed to watch, the aircraft remaining the property of the Italian Government and carrying Italian national markings. Once the aircraft were assembled, numerous demonstration flights were made, American officials being carried, as passengers, at the invitation of the Italians.

Early in September, the Aircraft Production Board began negotiations with Curtiss, as was normal prior to placing a formal order, with a view to their building the triplane. However, efforts to get the sample machine taken to Buffalo, and to obtain the necessary drawings to allow production, met with resistance by the Italians, and by October, although an order had been placed, Curtiss still had no information with which to begin. Over in France, Col. Bolling had several meetings with Maj. Perfetti, who had now returned from the US to try to resolve the apparent difficulty. Count Caproni himself attended one meeting and it was eventually agreed that the bombers could be fabricated in America and then shipped to France for assembly by Italian workmen. A site near Bordeaux was selected at which to do this.

However, although Bolling had recommended the triplane Ca.4 for short-range night bombing, and had requested that a sample be sent, on his return from Europe, Col. V. E. Clark recommended that the biplane be built instead. Then, on 19 September, a cable from France, No. 168, advised dropping the triplane from the programme and building 1,000 Caproni biplanes in their place. Although acting upon this advice appears to have taken some time, the order for Caproni triplanes was eventually cancelled and Curtiss given a new order for 500 Ca.5 biplanes, again with a new block of serial numbers. These machines were to be powered with Liberty engines, a design change that necessitated further revisions to the drawings, in addition to those needed to convert all measurements to units understood in America, and to suit American Standards. It would not be until some nine months after the Italian mission's first arrival in the US that all the drawings were received.

Then, on 30 October 1917, the Equipment Division informed the Aircraft Board that, in view of conditions at the front, the big bomber would not be made much use of and that the order should be reduced from 500 machines to just fifty. Curtiss were informed of the change, but were still awaiting drawings. The quantity ordered was later changed back to 500, although the new order was not actually issued until June 1918. Again, a new block of serial numbers was issued, but the entire order was formally cancelled after the Armistice without any machines being built.

An order had been placed with the Standard Aircraft Corporation, who were initially to build four prototypes, of which one each would be given to the Curtiss and Fisher Body companies as patterns upon which to base their own production. Unfortunately, the Standard Company, now owned by an investment syndicate, were experiencing management difficulties and progress was slower than had been hoped. When a representative of the Caproni Company visited Standard on 29 January 1918, they expected to find everything ready for production but instead discovered that little or nothing had been done.

By July, the situation was considered so serious that all the components for three of the prototypes were taken from Standard and given to Fisher Body for completion, along with further parts. The fourth prototype

A Caproni Ca5, purchased in Europe, in service in France.

machine, serial 42118, was almost complete and Standard were allowed to finish it, handing it over for acceptance tests, with test flying, following close inspection, beginning in September. Unfortunately, it was damaged by a fire on 2 October and was still undergoing repairs when the war ended.

Meanwhile, the Italian authorities, while retaining some mistrust of American business methods, realised that the project could have been managed better on their own part and the Caproni representatives in the US were brought under the control of the Italian Military Mission. The demonstration aircraft, which had arrived in the US in August 1917, was finally presented to the US Government in the summer of 1918, and was used to train crews in the operation of the type.

One example purchased from the Caproni Company was delivered to America in September 1918. This was for use by the US Navy in sea sled trials.

An order was also placed, as they appear to have wished all along, directly with the Caproni company, but only a few were delivered prior to the end of the war. These were unpopular with their America crews as they were fitted with 200-hp Fiat engines rather than the far more reliable 150-hp Isotta Fraschini engines that they would have preferred.

The Fisher Body Company found it necessary to redo some of the drawings before completing the machines started by Standard, although one was already about 85 per cent complete, and none were finished before the Armistice. The next completed aircraft was handed over on 21 November, followed by three more the following year. These stayed in service at least until 1921.

16

# Handley Page O/400

An agent from the Handley Page company, Mr W. Woodwork, arrived in the US on 4 May 1917, just a month after America's entry into the war. He sought to promote sales of the company's products, but there appears to have been no initial interest, possibly because, at that stage, America was thinking only of the tactical use of aeroplanes and not yet of strategic bombing. However, on his return from Europe in August 1917, Col. Clark recommended that the O/400 bomber should be added to the programme, a recommendation reinforced on 19 September by the same cable, No 168, which had advised that the Caproni triplane should be dropped.

At first, Handley Page demonstrated some reluctance to have their designs manufactured in America as the British Government had assured their new allies that all necessary data would be 'freely given'. However, on 9 December 1917, the company was assured that they would be suitably compensated, and thereafter co-operated more freely with companies in America.

The design of what became the Handley Page O/400 had begun late in 1914 in response to a request from RNAS for a machine to carry a worthwhile bombload. It was thus the company's first design for one of the huge aeroplanes for which they later became famous.

With a span of 100 feet, the wings were designed to fold so that the machine could be stored in sheds 75 feet square, and they were rigged in three bays. The prototype first flew on 17 December 1915, revealing that some modifications were required. These modifications, and some development essential to overcome problems in control, were completed by June 1916. The type, then the largest aeroplane ever built in England, entered service with the RNAS late in 1916 and began operations in March 1917. Later examples, with more powerful versions of the Rolls-Royce Eagle engine, served with the RFC/RAF as night bombers.

An example of the Handley Page O/400 flying low and probably coming in to land.

Handley Page O/400 in RFC service.

Handley Page O/400 C9704 with its wings folded so as to fit inside the hangars of the day.

A sample aeroplane and a full set of drawings were ordered for shipment to America, arriving in January 1918. On 26 January 1918, Brig.-Gen. Benjamin Foulois and the British Air Minister Lord Rothermere signed the 'Handley Page Agreement'. This enforced that the machines—which were too large to be shipped once assembled—would be fabricated in America, and the parts shipped to England for assembly and testing. Everything needed, except fabric and dope, was to be supplied by America, and it was intended that sufficient parts to assemble fifty aircraft would be shipped by May 1918, with a further shipment each week thereafter, and that the first US squadrons would be equipped with the big bomber by September. The number manufactured increased each month, and a total of thirty squadrons were in operation by the spring of 1919.

The site selected for erecting the bombers was near Oldham in Lancashire, where a newly completed, but still vacant cotton mill stood next to an open space suitable as an airfield, and where sufficient labour was available. The multi-storey mill, then named 'Gorse Mill No. 2', provided space for the assembly of components, but it was unsuited to the erection of the aeroplanes, for which purposes additional buildings were needed. On 1 March 1918, a contract to build a large factory building, six erecting sheds, eight hangars, and sundry office buildings was given to Trollop and Colls Ltd, who began work immediately. For both speed and economy, the buildings were constructed of a single skin of brick, reinforced by piers that also carried the roof loads. Although the factory building was completed, together with around 60 per cent of the erecting shed, most of the hangars were still under construction when the war ended. The site was to be run by the Alliance Aeroplane Company, a subsidiary of Waring & Gillow, who also managed the National Aeroplane factory at Aintree, and was handed over to them on 30 April in readiness for the expected arrival of parts for assembly. Clearing and levelling the airfield, which was to be the American Acceptance Park, was carried out by German POWs, but this was never fully completed.

The contract for the manufacture of components for 500 aircraft (serials 62445–62944) was placed with the Standard Aircraft Corporation, who in turn subcontracted much of the work out to other companies. Metal fittings were made by the Mullins Steel Boat Company of Salem, Ohio, and wooden components by the Grand Rapids Airplane Company, a consortium of furniture manufacturers.

Fifty machines were to be erected by Standard and retained in America for testing, development, and crew training, the rest being shipped to England. All were to be powered by the Liberty engine. The contract was not signed until 1 April 1918, although the programme had called for the first fifty sets of components, together with 125 Liberty engines, to be shipped to Liverpool by the beginning of May, followed by twice that number the next month, and three times as many in July.

Not surprisingly, the planned shipment schedule was not achieved, the first delivery, of just ten sets of components, not arriving in England until late August. These were followed by thirty sets in September and sixty more in October. A further thirty sets were shipped but arrived after the Armistice. In addition, seven Handley Page O/400s had been erected in America, the first of these making its initial flight on 1 July, although it is possible that this was actually the sample aeroplane shipped over from England, fitted with Liberty engines. Whatever its origins, it was proudly named 'Langley' in a ceremony conducted by the wife of the Standard Company's President before giving a demonstration flight in front of a large audience. This machine, together with others assembled in America, continued in service, mostly conducting bomb-dropping trials and giving demonstration flights, until 1923.

In England, just three machines had been completely assembled by the time of the Armistice, with four further fuselages partially assembled and work in progress on a few more. These machines appear to have been dismantled; their parts and all the unassembled components were repacked and shipped back to the US, with surprising despatch, the last of them leaving Liverpool by the end of January 1919.

The assembly buildings at Oldham were demolished, and in 1919, the mill, now renamed Ace Mill, began weaving cotton. The large factory building was also retained and is still extant.

The Handley Page O/400 Langley with crossed flags painted on its nose.

Langley being recovered after a minor mishap in which it tipped over and damaged its nose.

# 17

# Martin MB-1

Late in 1917, the newly formed Glenn L. Martin Company began work on a large bomber, with a crew of three, designed to replace the Handley Page O/400. The new machine was somewhat smaller than its rival, with a wing span on just over 71 feet. It was otherwise similar in layout, with twin engines mounted between the equal span wings, and with twin fins and rudders. Glenn Martin was an experienced designer, having first started in business in 1912, then going into partnership with the Wright Company to form Wright-Martin before staring up his own company again in September 1917.

An order for six examples of the new machine was placed, off the drawing board, on 17 January 1918, with the serial numbers 39055–39060 allocated to them. The first aircraft, completed for observation rather than bombing, flew in October 1918, but it was nonetheless designated GMB, for Glenn Martin Bomber. Three more were handed over, equipped for the observation role, with only the final two being completed as bombers, a role for which the ending of the war immediately removed any immediate need.

The type was developed as the MB-1 bomber, and also as the MB-2 torpedo carrier, which, after twenty were ordered by the US Navy in June 1920, was renamed the MT, for Martin Torpedo.

Other variants included the 1,500-mile-range GMT (Transcontinental), the GMC that was fitted with a 37-mm cannon in its nose, and the GMP that seated ten passengers in an enclosed cabin. None of these variants entered volume production, and the original machines found employment as with the government-run air mail service.

A Martin MB-1 is handed over to the air service in October 1918. The type was completed too late to see active service in the war. (*US Air Force Photo*)

18

# De Havilland D.H.4

Following its inclusion as an advanced trainer in the Aircraft Production Board's preliminary proposals, published on 13 June 1917, a sample machine (probably A7531) provided with neither engine nor armament was shipped aboard SS *Adriatic* and arrived in New York on 18 July. By 27 July, it was in Washington DC, where it was reviewed by a number of senior officers and government officials. By 15 August, it had been taken to McCook Field, Dayton, Ohio, for technical evaluation by the Engineering Division.

The D.H.4 was a two-seat day bomber designed for the Aircraft Manufacturing Company by Geoffrey de Havilland. It made its first flight, piloted by its designer, in August 1917, following which, it underwent the normal process of testing and development. A number of different engines were tried, the best of which was the Rolls-Royce Eagle, although demand for this engine for other aircraft types was already high and far exceeded the supply available. The D.H.4 was already in service when the Bolling Mission toured Europe, and although already approaching obsolescence, it was included in their recommendations as the day bomber best suited for production in America, including it in preliminary proposals sent by cable before leaving England, as well as in Bolling's final report. However, on 30 July, Gen. Pershing noted that changes would need to be made to the design of the D.H.4 in order to increase its bombload. Yet on 2 August, Bolling cabled to say that the makers had already made the necessary improvements in a new model designated the D.H.9.

Generally similar in design to the D.H.4, the D.H.9 answered one of the criticisms of the earlier design by having the two cockpits close together, those in the D.H.4 being separated by the fuel tank that—although it placed this disposable load at the aircraft's centre of gravity,

A British built D.H.9. Orders were placed for its mass production in America before it was decided to revert to the earlier and more effective D.H.4.

thus eliminating trim problems—made communication between pilot and observer difficult. The introduction of D.H.9 also overcame the difficulties created by the shortage in supplies of the Rolls-Royce Eagle engine, being intended to be powered by a new B.H.P. engine rated at 300 hp. Though this was then still under development, it was of little consequence to the Americans, who planned to fit the Liberty anyway.

On 5 September, the Aircraft Production Board recommended placing orders for 2,000 examples of the DH9, a quantity that Col. Bolling suggested by cable from Europe should be doubled. The design needed to be modified in order to fit American armament, instruments, and, of course, the Liberty engine, as well as reproducing all the manufacturing drawings to suit American methods, measurements, and material standards. Nonetheless, on 8 October, an order for 2,000 was placed with Dayton-Wright. Then, later the same month, this quantity was increased to 3,750, together with 250 D.H.4s to be used as advanced trainers, an order for 3,000 D.H.9s being given to Fisher Body the same day. The Board also recommended that orders be placed with Fisher Body for 1,000 extra D.H.9 fuselages and 1,500 sets of wings, as spares, to be used in the field. An order for 500 was also placed with the Standard Aeroplane Corporation, although the contract was not signed until January 1918.

Meanwhile, the sample D.H.4 was fitted with a prototype Liberty engine and made its first flight from McCook Field on 29 October 1917, beginning the process of testing and development.

Development of the D.H.9 also took its time, with a host of teething troubles slowing production and with problems with the B.H.P. engine necessitating it being down-rated to 230 hp before it would run reliably. By 25 January 1918, when only five D.H.9s had been completed by manufacturers in England, it became clear to the Aircraft Board that the design was not yet sufficiently well-established to allow it to be reproduced by America's mass production methods and the substitution of the D.H.4, which was a well-proven design, was recommended instead. All contracts to build the D.H.9 were therefore cancelled and replaced with new contracts for similar numbers of D.H.4s, although all the necessary paperwork to amend the contracts was not completed until 29 March 1918. The cost per aircraft, not including engine, instruments, or armament, was set at $5,500 (then £1,100), plus the allowed profit of around 20 per cent, which tends to confirm the efficiency of American mass production methods as the equivalent cost for the British built version was £1,424 10*s*.

In April, a further revised production plan showed that the DH-4, as the Americans designated the design, had been reclassified as a combat aircraft rather than an advanced trainer. It was planned for it to equip forty-four day-bombing squadrons and a further twenty-four observation squadrons.

A request to retain the first fifty machines completed in the US as trainers, and so that 'they can be closely observed and the benefit of any troubles or necessary corrections be immediately given to manufacturers', was rejected. Gen. Pershing responded that just five should be retained in the US and every other available aeroplane be sent to France as soon as possible.

February 1918 had seen the first few examples of the DH-4 from the batch of 250 originally ordered from Dayton-Wright completed and handed over to the US Army, the first being shipped to France, from Hoboken, on 15 March 1918; it made its initial flight in France on 17 May, after it had been fitted with instruments and armament. This, however, was a mere gesture, with volume production not beginning until May, when 153 were completed, and shipment, in quantity, starting in July. No machine was made available for official testing until April 1918, after the first production example had already been shipped to France, and on 24 April, a full-throttle endurance test had to be abandoned after 102 minutes when the radiator

An unidentified DH-4 in service with the Signal Corps.

shutters broke due to excessive vibration and the auxiliary fuel tank began leaking. A similar test, conducted the next day, was abandoned after five sparking plugs had failed. On 2 May, the test machine spun to the ground from a height of around 300 feet, killing the crew (Maj. Oscar Brindley and Lt-Col. Henry Damm), although the cause of the crash was more likely to have been pilot error than any fault with the machine.

On 2 August, the 135th Aero Squadron went into action as an observation unit, and later in the month, Newton Baker, the Secretary of War, interviewed with the press:

> I have a cablegram from Gen. Pershing which tells me that early in the present month of August a complete squadron of American made De Havilland 4 planes, with Liberty engines, conducted a reconnaissance back of German lines and successfully returned without loss. Gen. Foulois personally led the expedition.

By the end of the war, the 135th had been joined by the 8th, 50th, 85th, 91st, 133rd, 168th, 278th, and 354th Observation Squadrons and the 11th, 20th, 100th, and 163rd Day Bombing Squadrons, although some of these units did not reach the front until just weeks, or even days, before the Armistice, and several never saw action at all.

Thirty-seven American-built DH-4s were lost in action, with a further 249 written-off in accidents. A total of fifty-nine combat victories were claimed by DH-4 crews. At the date of the Armistice, 196 were actually in service at the front, shared between the twelve squadrons then operational.

American experiences in France demonstrated the same problems that the British had found: crew communication was difficult, the two cockpits being separated by the fuel tank, and the machine was nose heavy when landing. Although the fuel tank was designed to be self-sealing if punctured by a bullet, a rumour grew that the DH-4 was likely to catch fire when attacked, and although statistics show that, on average, it was actually less likely to do so than some other types then in service, it acquired the nickname 'The Flying Coffin'. However, this was much in keeping with the grim humour of the time, such macabre appellations being common.

In order to overcome some of these problems, a revised variant, the DH-4B, was designed towards the end of 1918, in which the fuel tank was moved forward, the pilot being placed behind it, bringing the two cockpits together as in the D.H.9, thereby improving not only crew communication, but also the pilot's view. The undercarriage was redesigned, moving the wheels forward to cure the nose-over problem, and the fuselage sides were entirely covered with plywood.

By the end of hostilities, around 3,200 DH-4s had been completed and handed over to the Army, with a total with over 1,000 more being completed by the time production was finally stopped (see Appendix II).

The DH-4B introduced revised crew positions and greatly improved crew communication. This example is preserved in the USAF Museum in Dayton, Ohio.

With many of the recently completed machines still in America, waiting to be shipped to Europe, there were more than enough to fulfil its peacetime needs without bringing home all those already in France, especially as all available shipping space was needed to bring home the troops, and many were destroyed in what the press described as 'a billion dollar bonfire'.

Post-war, many, if not all of the original DH-4s that had been retained in service in America were converted to DH-4Bs, the contracts for the conversion being placed in small batches with a number of companies, including Aeromarine, Boeing, Curtiss, Dayton-Wright, Gallaudet, LWF, and Thomas Morse, helping to keep the industry in existence at a time when orders for new aeroplanes were scarce. Thus modified, the DH-4B remained in service with the US Army until 1931.

The type was also employed in flying the mail, a specially modified variant being developed with a single cockpit slightly further aft behind both the fuel tank and a mail locker.

A number survive in museums in the US to this day, while a number of recent reproductions can occasionally be seen at air shows.

DH-4s modified for carrying air mail with the pilot's cockpit moved aft to accommodate a locker for the mail.

19

# USD-9

In the spring of 1918, with the design of the D.H.9 as finalised as ever a machine of war could be, efforts were made (first in England and then in the US) to fit it with the Liberty engine, thereby gaining all its advantages over the earlier D.H.4, such as improved crew communication, while overcoming the power shortfall of its current engine. England had ordered 3,000 Liberty engines to be delivered at the rate of 500 per month starting in January 1918, but by March, they had received just ten. Geoffrey de Havilland, at the Aircraft Manufacturing Company, was busy with new projects, and the development of the new machine, designated D.H.9A, was entrusted to Westland Aircraft Ltd who produced a strengthened machine with bigger wings and a Liberty engine that entered service, in small numbers, in the summer of 1918.

In America, where the new design, initially designated USD-9, was intended to replace the DH-4 in both observation and bombing roles, the work was undertaken by the Signal Corps' Engineering Division. They modified the British design quite extensively, changing the wing section and reducing the stagger, as well as fitting a completely new fuel system. Construction of three prototypes was well advanced by early July, when a weekly report on the Division's activities noted that the type was to be redesignated USD-9A to parallel the English version, this being their only acknowledgment of any contribution to the design from outside America.

Testing of the first example began on 20 July at McCook Field, although no serial number appears to have even been assigned to it. The two further examples built by the Engineering Division were given the serials 40026 and 40027. At least four more examples, 40060–40063, were built by the Engineering Division, and one—designated USD-9B, with an increased

The USD-9A was intended to be an improvement on the DH-4. This example was retained for testing at McCook Field and never saw service.

USD-9A SC40062, which was shipped to Europe on 4 November, its fate being unrecorded in the confusion and celebration of the ending of the war.

wing area to improve its bomb-carrying capacity—was almost complete by the ending of hostilities

Three had been ordered from Fisher Body simply to verify that the Engineering Division's drawings were sufficient for production, but the order had to be cancelled when the company's design engineer left.

Six USD-9As were therefore ordered from Dayton-Wright (who were also building the structurally similar DH-4). The first was completed by 19 August 1918 and delivered for testing at McCook Field by September, where the number P43 was assigned to it and was eventually painted on its rudder. During testing, a larger rudder, with a more rounded trailing edge, was designed. This was intended to replace the original design on production examples.

The type was approved for production on 18 October, with one example already having been delivered to Curtiss as a pattern, with whom an order for 4,000 was placed on 1 November. This was later cancelled after the Armistice, with none being completed.

The third and fourth USD-9As completed by Dayton-Wright were crated for shipping to Europe, with 40062 sailing from New York on 4 November 1918 and 40063 following three days later. What happened to them on arrival, after the end of hostilities, is unrecorded.

With the coming of peace, the USD-9A was abandoned, budget restrictions preventing the acquisition of new aeroplanes for some time, and its intended roles continued to be carried out by the DH-4s it had been designed to replace.

20

# LUSAC-11

In January 1918, an experienced French aeronautical engineer, *Capitaine* Georges Lepère, joined the Packard Company in Detroit to collaborate on the design of an aircraft specifically for mass production in American factories. This was to be powered by the V12 Liberty engine. The resulting design was the Lepère United States Army Combat design No. 11, or LUSAC-11, which was intended to undertake the roles of reconnaissance and light bombing, while being well able to defend itself, rather in the style of the Bristol Fighter. It was therefore to be fitted with twin forward-firing Marlin machine guns, and with twin Lewis guns mounted on a Scarff ring for defence.

It was intended to be simple to manufacture and easy to maintain, and it featured one-piece inter-plane struts of laminated spruce in a rhomboid shape, which eliminated the need for cross bracing between the wings. Conventional landing and flying wires were retained, but the staggered wings were rigged without dihedral to simplify erection. The fuselage sides were covered with plywood for rigidity, further reducing the amount of wire bracing that its erection required. However, although this made erection and maintenance easier, it rendered repair to any damage far more complicated.

An unusual six-strut undercarriage was provided for strength and rigidity.

The first prototype was completed by the end of April 1918 and taken Wilbur Wright Field, near Dayton, where testing began on 15 May. Its first flight appears to have been made by a French officer, Lt de Marmier, although it was also test flown by a number of pilots from nearby McCook Field. Although engine problems necessitated a forced-landing during the initial flight, reports were generally favourable with a maximum speed of 136 mph being recorded.

LUSAC-11 SC40116 showing the unusual inter-plane struts that eliminated the need for cross bracing between the wings.

In addition to the three prototypes (40015–40017), a further batch of twenty-five (42128–42152) was ordered from Packard, and plans were made to place orders for thousands more. The production versions differed from the prototypes by having a slight increase in wing span, from 39 feet to 41 feet 7 inches, a change that improved lifting capacity, but reduced the maximum speed at ground level to 132 mph. In addition, the ailerons were modified and the fuel feed system revised.

The first production machine, 42128, was handed over to the Air Service in September, and three were shipped to France, 42130 and 42131, going to the A.E.F's Technical Section at Orly, where they arrived on 17 October. No. 42133 was handed over to the French for evaluation, who had a view to also operate the type.

Following erection, the first machine at Orly was flight tested on 5 November, piloted by Lt de Marmier, who had accompanied it on its trans-Atlantic journey. Completion of the machine had been delayed by a shortage of rigging wires and clevis pins among the parts shipped from America, and suitable alternatives had to be sourced locally. The official report on the tests stated that, although all the pilots who had flown the 'Lepère' thought that it handled exceptionally well, almost every flight

This LUSAC-11, SC42129, has been painted with the simple camouflage scheme being introduced towards the end of the war.

Another camouflaged LUSAC-11 clearly showing the unusual sturdy undercarriage.

encountered difficulties either with the fuel feed or the cooling system. Test flights in the US revealed similar problems, and although it was accepted that these problems could probably be resolved by further development, it was eventually concluded that 'even had the defects noted been eliminated, this plane would not have ultimately shown sufficient superiority in performance and general design over the further advanced DH-4 and USD-9a planes, to justify adding it to the list for production'.

Although only seven had been completed by the time of the Armistice, the whole batch of twenty-five was built. Further orders, which had been placed late in October with Packard (1,000), Fisher Body (1,000), and Brewster (500), were cancelled.

At least one of the thirty-one machines completed served with the US Navy and remained in use until 1927. The remainder were mainly used for testing and development, one being fitted with a turbocharged engine and reaching an altitude of 33,114 feet on 27 February 1920, piloted by Capt. R. W. Schroeder—a record increased to 39,700 feet by Lt J. A. Macready the following year.

LUSAC-11 P53 fitted with a turbocharged Liberty engine. It eventually reached an altitude of 39,700 feet, the pilot using oxygen and a special heated flying suit.

Three further examples, designated the LUSAC-21, were completed after the Armistice. These were for testing, and they were fitted with the Bugatti King engine, a revised version of a sixteen-cylinder engine originally designed in France by Bugatti, but modified by Col. C. B. King and manufactured by the Duesenberg Motor Corporation. It was not a great success and only about forty were completed before production was halted.

21

# Growing Dissatisfaction

In the first months of 1918, the Aircraft Board were still assuring the War Department that the aeroplanes would be delivered as promised, the Secretary of War therefore giving similar assurances to the nation and issuing the following, slightly misleading, statement on 21 February:

> The first American built battle planes are today en route to the front in France, This first shipment, though in itself not large, marks the final overcoming of the many difficulties met in building up this new and intricate industry.
>
> These planes are equipped with the first Liberty motor from machine production. One of them in a recent test surpassed all records for speed and climbing for planes of that type.
>
> Engine production, which began a month ago, is now on a quantity basis and the peak of production will be reached in a few weeks.

'Not large' was a mastery of understatement as only a handful of DH-4s had been completed by that date and the shipment comprised a single aircraft. Nor would engine production approach a 'peak of production' until late April.

However, by the spring, it had become increasingly obvious both to the US Government and to many members of the public that, despite these morale-boosting statements, all was not going to plan. The production programme, as produced on 4 October 1917, had called for 2,665 aeroplanes, all built in America, to be at the front by 1 April 1918, a figure already well below that required by the Ribot Proposal. Later programmes had revised this figure, first to 2,870 and then back up to 4,027, but when 1 April 1918 came, not one single American-built aeroplane was in action, or even at the front.

By 1 April 1918, only 253 Liberty engines had been delivered, 122 being allocated for Army aeroplanes, the remainder going to the Navy. However, well over 3,000 primary trainers, mostly either Curtiss JN-4s or Standard J-1s, had been delivered.

The first investigation into the conduct of the programme appears to have been that instigated by Gutzon de la Mothe Borglum, the sculptor later famous as the creator of the huge monument depicting past presidents at Mount Rushmore, who considered himself an expert on aeronautics. In September 1917, Borglum had approached the Aircraft Production Board with an offer to supply eighty aeroplanes of literally incredible performance. When his offer was rejected, he complained to the White House, accusing the Board of mismanagement. Told by an official to put his complaint in writing, Borglum did so, and in December 1917, he recommended that President Wilson should appoint a commission, headed by Borglum, to investigate the procurement process. The President, who was well aware of Borglum's reputation for controversy, made a non-committal response that the sculptor interpreted as approval, preparing a report in which the whole programme was strongly criticised; Edward Deeds was singled out as the main target, with Borglum claiming that he had shown favouritism to his friends and business colleagues. This animosity was, perhaps, understandable as Deeds, along with other prominent citizens of Dayton, Ohio, had in 1912 commissioned Borglum to design a memorial to Wilbur Wright, the project later being cancelled after the city was devastated by a flood.

However, when Borglum submitted his report to the President, it was ignored and so he took it instead to the *New York Herald* newspaper, which published it in two instalments during March 1918. In view of the accusation of profiteering and corruption thus made public, the President felt compelled to act and appointed Charles E. Hughes, a former presidential candidate and Supreme Court judge, to head an official investigation into the allegations.

Also in March, Walter S. Gifford, Director of the Council of National Defense, became temporary Director of the Aircraft Board, and on 24 April, John D. Ryan, a copper magnate, took over the position. The following month, the newly created Bureau of Aircraft Production, headed by Ryan, took over the duties of the Aircraft Board. Edward Deeds' involvement was thus terminated.

Two members of the US Government, Congressman F. H. LaGuardia and Senator Morris Sheppard, had previously jointly proposed that a Department of Aeronautics should be set up to take control of the whole programme, but their bill had died in committee, without ever being debated. Nonetheless, such a board was now created, headed by Gen. Kenly, as part of the restructuring process.

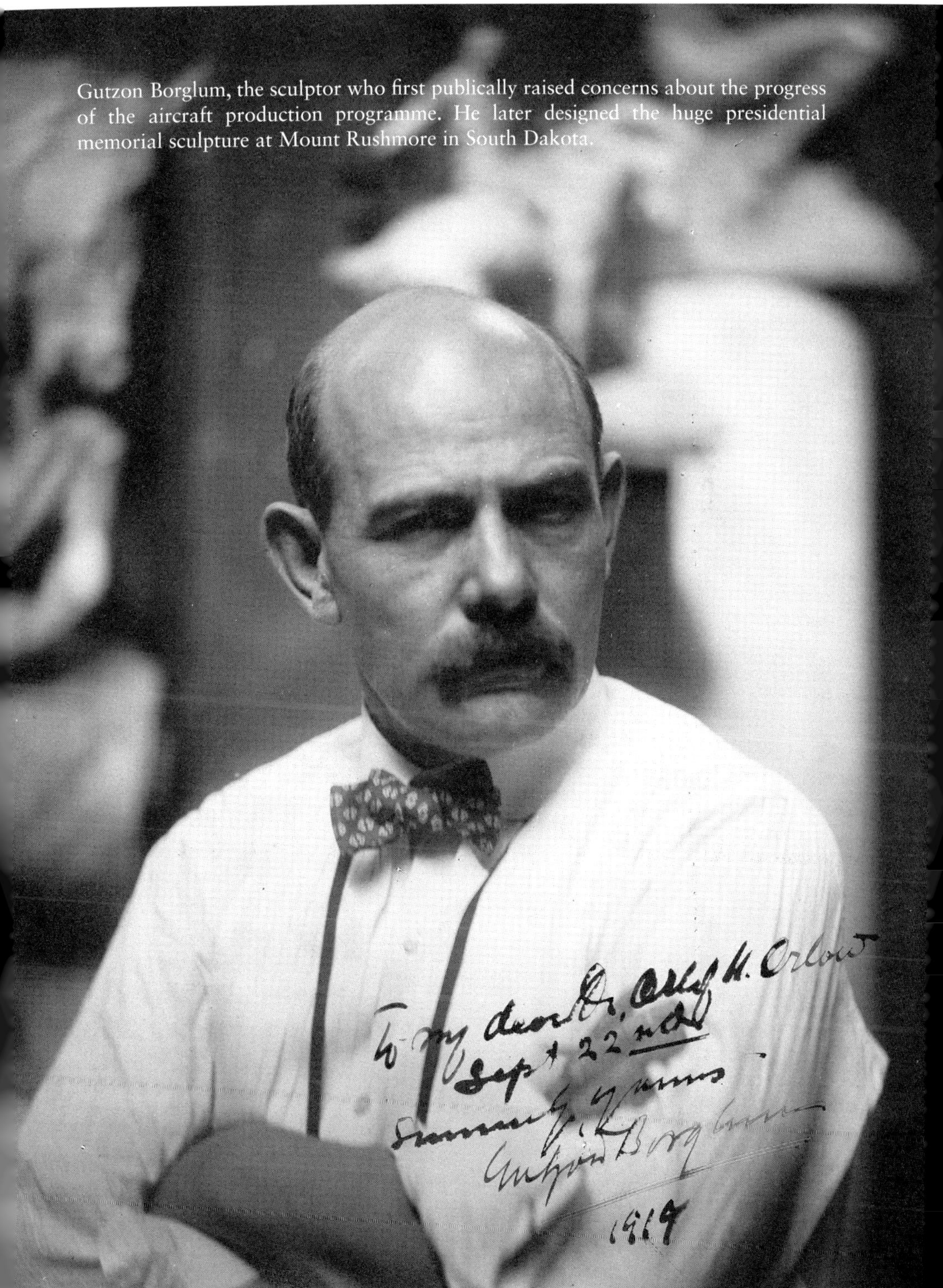


Gutzon Borglum, the sculptor who first publically raised concerns about the progress of the aircraft production programme. He later designed the huge presidential memorial sculpture at Mount Rushmore in South Dakota.

On 30 April 1918, the US Senate voted to initiate its own investigation into the management of the programme, to be carried out by the Committee of Military Affairs who appointed a subcommittee for the purpose on 29 May. These two official enquiries were conducted independently, with differing terms of reference, and were allowed equal access to official records. Each examined numerous witnesses, a total of 250 in the case of the Senate's investigation, although the number interviewed by the department of Justice enquiry, chaired by Charles Hughes, is less well recorded. The witnesses examined included representatives of aeroplane manufacturers, inspectors, pilots, and military personnel, as well as Deeds and Squier.

Grover Loening, who had managed the Wright Company during 1913–14 before founding his own aeroplane company, complained to the investigators that smaller companies, like his own, which had experience of aeroplane building and were easily capable of expansion, had not been granted government contracts, while newly formed businesses, without previous experience, had been given large orders. Witteman-Lewis of New Jersey was pointed out to the Senate investigation as another established aeroplane building company that had been denied any military orders, as had many others.

Orville Wright was also among the many witnesses interviewed by the Hughes investigation, but explained that he was merely employed by the Dayton-Wright company as a salaried consultant, that his position was entirely non-executive, and that he owned no stock, thereby divorcing himself from the company's business affairs. In practice, this was entirely fair as his position was a sinecure, his name being his most important and, very probably, only contribution to the company's affairs. His attendance was required only for occasional publicity purposes, such as when he posed for a photograph with a newly completed DH-4.

One result of these various enquiries into the progress of the programme appears to have been a considerable increase in publicity, put out by aeroplane manufacturers, to increase public consciousness of what they had achieved. Photographs of factory interiors, with large numbers of aeroplanes under manufacture, were produced, although, in those days of careful poses and slow shutter speeds, these must have had a severely adverse effect on production, whatever their benefit to morale. Even more time consuming were photographs of assembled components, arranged in neat formations, to illustrate the results of a day's or a week's production in that particular plant.

In view of the urgency with which aeroplanes were needed in France, some of the companies that were new to aeroplane production, such as Fisher Body and Dayton-Wright, adopted the quality control methods common in mass production, taking random samples of components for

Employees pose with completed DH-4 fuselages in the vast Fisher Body works. Such images, intended to illustrate the efficiency of production and the extent of output, were suddenly common as the investigations into the aircraft building programme took place.

inspection rather than the close examination of every part as was more usual to the aircraft industry. It appears probable that only one aeroplane in five was submitted for examination, or even test flown, As a result, it was almost inevitable that a few faulty machines made it into service, leading to rumours of faulty workmanship, which further reduced confidence in both the programme and its products.

The Senate Committee's nineteen-page report, published on 22 August 1918, confirmed that the programme had indeed been mismanaged and that some profit margins had been excessive. In addition, it was discovered that some components rejected after inspection had nonetheless been paid for, instead of their cost being borne by the manufacturer concerned. While the report conceded that Detroit, with its abundance of automobile factory space, was a sensible choice as a manufacturing centre, it criticised the selection of Dayton, which offered no such advantages.

A DH-4 ready for testing at Dayton Wright's South Field. Only one in every five completed machines was tested, which speeded delivery to the front, but allowed faults to pass unnoticed.

Once aeroplanes were completed, delivery to France was slowed by the adoption of Dayton, Ohio, as the hub of operations, a huge warehouse having been built there at a cost of $500,000, with materials manufactured in factories near the east coast having to be transported inland to Dayton for acceptance and then transported back east for shipping overseas.

Newton Baker, Secretary of War, was found not to have deliberately misled the Government, and thus the people, over the progress of the programme, but had himself been misled by those in charge of it. Although the committee had not directly investigated the allegations of corruption made by Borglum, it did note that Deeds, although having divested himself of his business interests in companies accepting government contracts, had shown favouritism to former associates and had centred activities in his hometown of Dayton. The report also suggested that much of the money appropriated by Congress had been wasted, with many millions spent on abortive attempts to fit the Liberty engine into the Bristol Fighter and the SPAD, as well as on constructing over 1,200 Standard J-1 trainers that were subsequently grounded.

Liberty engines ready for installation in the DH-4s being built at the Fisher Body factory.

These conclusions were widely reported, although in suitably edited form, and appeared in both national and local newspapers not only in the US but throughout the British Empire, with details published as far afield as Australia and New Zealand within a week of their being made public in America.

The Hughes report, commissioned by the President specifically to investigate allegations of corruption, was not made public immediately. It strongly criticised Deeds for steering the award of contracts towards his friends, and for giving business advice while employed by the government; however, it brought no actual charges against him. It also cited examples of favouritism and of mismanagement by Deeds, and suggested that, as an army officer, he should be court-martialled.

However, the Army, having already completed restructured its aviation section and being anxious to play down the situation as much as was possible, chose not to bring any charges against him, and concentrated instead on fighting the war.

Apart from the obvious adverse effect upon the nation's morale, these allegations and investigations seem to have had no material effect on the aircraft building program, with output from the various factories finally beginning to gather momentum.

22

# The Air Service 'Over There'

When America first entered the war in April 1917, many people—among both her new allies and their enemies—considered that she would not be able to enlist, train, and equip an army of any great size and then ship it to Europe. Gen. Joffre, in command of France's Army, expected their contribution might extend to perhaps 500,000 men, and Germany initially expected even fewer. Indeed, the Aeronautical Section's original proposals had been based on such a modest force, but later, a plan to field at least eighty divisions (approximately 1.5 million men) by the spring of 1919 evolved.

Not only would a vast fleet of ships be required to transport this force and its equipment to France, but Germany's campaign of unrestricted submarine warfare, with some of their newest boats able to operate right across the Atlantic, approaching the shores of the USA, was making the ocean crossing increasingly hazardous. In November 1917, the Aircraft Board declared: 'All measures taken against submarines should have precedence over all other measures'. They also advocated that priority should be given to the requirements of the Navy.

At first, France and Germany's predictions seemed to have been proved correct as, by early 1918, only 175,000 American soldiers had reached France, and a Shipping Control Committee, chaired by Mr P. Franklin, had been formed to oversee the movement of men and equipment across the Atlantic; this was to ensure the best possible use of the shipping capacity available. There was never sufficient capacity to ship everything required, and the committee constantly sought to find a balance to transport enough of each different commodity to fulfil immediate needs and so ensure that the US Army in France was never deprived of some essential supplies. At the same time, the committee also strove to make the best possible use of the ships on their return journey, bringing back materials (such as African mahogany, which was used to make propellers) that could not be supplied from within the United States.

On 21 March 1918, Germany, in a final attempt to win the war before the arrival of any greater numbers of American troops, began a huge advance, and it became paramount that the Allies fielded sufficient manpower to resist and then repel this advance. Priority was therefore given to transporting ground forces and their associated equipment to the combat area, with little or no shipping space left for anything else. The few aeroplanes that had been completed had to remain in America until space could be found to begin shipping them to France, and it was not until 11 May 1918 that the first American-built aeroplane arrived in France.

Expansion of the Air Service presented no less of a challenge, for although new flying training stations were rapidly built, the tiny pre-war Aeronautical Section possessed few qualified instructors who could teach new recruits the skills required. In the case of aircrew, the problem was partially overcome by retaining the first batches of newly qualified pilots at the flying schools to teach the next intake of pupils. In addition, many student pilots were sent to Europe for training in flying schools in England and France. The 85th Aero Squadron, for example, spent five months training at Harlaxton, near Grantham in Lincolnshire, under supervision by the RFC before moving to France.

As in other countries, ground crew were initially recruited from among those workers who already had appropriate skills, such as carpenters and motor mechanics. A publicity campaign was introduced to encourage them to volunteer for the Air Service before they could be conscripted into the ground forces, meaning that their skills were lost to the units that needed them most.

The 1st Aero Squadron arrived at Le Havre on 2 September 1917, but this was a unit of the original Signal Corps' Aeronautical Section—veterans of the Mexico campaign—and it was not until January 1918 that the first squadron composed mainly of newly recruited personnel arrived in France, going first to the depot at St Maxient.

Some Air Service personnel, both air and ground crew, were attached to British and French units so as to gain practical experience with some pilots even going into action with their hosts.

For a long time, the Americans were heavily reliant on their allies for various kinds of supplies and spare parts, as well as for aeroplanes, and never became entirely self-sufficient as it was obviously simpler, and more efficient, to source such commodities locally, whenever possible, rather than ship them across the Atlantic from America.

On 7 February, as the first DH-4s began to be completed in Detroit, Col. Sidney D. Waldon sent a cable to Gen. Foulois requesting that the first

*Above:* Crews of the 11th Aero Squadron pose with their DH-4s for a photographer whose own shadow can be seen in the foreground.

*Below:* Youthful-looking mechanics with a Liberty powered DH-4.

fifty examples completed be assigned to aircrew training. The reply, sent over Gen. Pershing's name, demanded instead that if fifty were available, forty-five should be shipped to France and just five retained for training. While the need for additional air support in France was understandable, this attitude, which was widespread throughout the AEF, meant that many pilots had little or no experience of service aircraft before reaching a squadron in France. Waldon's acknowledgement, cabled a week later, pointed out that the aircraft then available still lacked instruments and guns, and it was some time before the first machine ever left for France.

The first American Pursuit Squadron, No. 94, flew its first active service patrol on 14 April 1918, equipped with aeroplanes purchased from the French, adopting the famous 'Hat in the Ring' marking. Throughout the remainder of the war, the US would purchase many aircraft from the French, as previously arranged by the Bolling Mission, including Nieuport and SPAD fighters, together with Breguet and Salmson bombing and reconnaissance machines, which would operate alongside the American-built DH-4s; these began operations on 2 August 1918.

Officers of the 8th Aero Squadron pose with one of the squadron's DH-4s.

Some very young-looking enlisted men, plus a couple of commissioned officers of the 8th Aero Squadron.

23

# The Situation at the End of the War

By November 1918, America's aeroplane building industry had expanded almost beyond recognition; capable only of producing a few hundred aeroplanes each year in 1916, it could now turn out up to ten times that number every month. Production capacity was still expanding when the cessation of hostilities brought demand for new aeroplanes to a sudden halt and may have already reached the point where it exceeded the nation's capacity to ship them overseas as fast as they could be built.

The first DH-4 had arrived in France in May 1918 and a total of 3,431 had been completed by 11 November, the majority either having been shipped to France or being in transit. Yet wastage was high and, as with all other combat types, nothing like this number were still in action or even available for operational use.

The 20th Aero Squadron, typical of many American units, received its first DH-4 on 29 August 1918, and over the remainder of the war, they were assigned a total of sixty-six machines in order to maintain an active force of eighteen. Of these sixty-six aircraft, five were lost in action and at least sixteen were sufficiently damaged either by enemy action or in accidents. These were returned to the depot for salvage, along with at least nine others that were also returned to the depot for unspecified reasons.

The situation with regard to aero engines was very similar. Of the 15,572 twelve-cylinder Liberty engines recorded as having been delivered up to the Armistice, 5,323 had been allocated to companies building aeroplanes for the US Army, but a further 4,311 had been assigned to the AEF in France as spares. Of the remainder, 907 went to training units, 3,742 to the US Navy, and 1,089 to America's allies, including Britain, partially in exchange for combat aeroplanes.

*Above:* The Buick factory standing idle on 20 November 1918, all manufacturing having ceased with the Armistice.

*Below:* Incomplete flying boats in the final assembly bay of the Curtiss Aeroplane and Motor Company's North Elmwood Plant, Buffalo, New York, on 11 November 1918.

French-built SPAD S.XIII fighters of the 213th Aero Squadron on 11 November 1918.

DH-4 of the 96th Aero Squadron.

A total of well over 5,000 aircraft were supplied to America's Air Service by her allies and, indeed, the majority of the aeroplanes operated in France by American Air Service squadrons were not manufactured in the US. These included 496 Nieuports, 705 Salmsons, and 1,090 SPADs. Although only 196 US-built DH-4s were in active service at the end of the war, her front-line strength totalled approximately 750 aircraft.

By the end of the war, 4,307 American flyers were stationed in France, with a further 7,118 in the US, although many of the latter were still under training. These numbers, although well short of either those required by the various expansion plans, still represented a considerable achievement.

Realising that unfulfilled orders would inevitably be cancelled once the war had ended, some companies endeavoured to complete as many aircraft as possible, mass producing components so as to maximise their profit before peace brought production to a halt.

The 12th Aero Squadron at its base in Arizona in 1920, still equipped with DH-4s.

The 166th Aero Squadron line-up in front of its DH-4s in November 1918.

# Conclusions

Obviously, America's aeroplane building programme was far from being a total success, having been mismanaged from the start. But where did it succeed, and in what areas did it fail and why?

Manufacture of aircraft for training purposes was the most successful aspect of the programme, with production of primary trainers meeting the proposed programme and adequately fulfilling the Army's needs. Construction of these aircraft and their engines was carried out to existing, proven designs largely by companies established prior to America's entry into the war and already familiar with aircraft manufacture.

The Liberty was produced in considerable numbers by companies already producing thousands of engines each year to power their automobiles. However, the design was not fully developed at the time it was committed to production, and the consequent detail changes prevented output ever reaching the industry's full capacity, with production still expanding right up to the cessation of hostilities.

The greatest disappointment was, most unfortunately, with the flagship of the whole programme: the DH-4. The plan had required that 2,500 would have been built as advanced trainers, together with 12,000 for operational use by 31 July 1918. However, only 8,500 had actually been ordered by that date, 1,000 had been completed, and just 641 embarked for shipment to France, with only sixty-seven having reached the front.

The $640 million that had been appropriated to cover the cost of the aircraft building programme to August 1918 proved insufficient, especially with the wastage on cancelled projects; further funds had been needed. The wave of patriotic fervour, which saw the initial appropriation bill pass through Congress almost without question, had dissipated,

The 1,000th DH-4 completed ready to be shipped to France at a time when the programme had called for many thousands more to already be in active service

but the spiralling cost of the war had made the sums involved appear less significant, with, for example, $762 million spent on artillery shells. Further appropriations were made, with an additional $1,051, 511,980 being allocated to cover the period up to June 1919. Of course, the war ended on 11 November 1918 before it had all been spent, although some cancellation charges had still to be paid, and the total sum finally expended on Military Aviation during the war period was in the region of $1,200 million.

The programme's area of greatest success, in the building of training aircraft, showed what could be done by adopting existing, fully developed designs and entrusting their manufacture to established companies familiar with aeroplanes. Production of those designs could then also be undertaken by companies new to aircraft production, initially under supervision, with both Fisher Body and Dayton-Wright successfully fulfilling their contracts to build such machines.

With regard to the less successful areas of the programme, both the contemporary investigations and subsequent appraisals all broadly agree that the shortcomings were caused by four contributory causes:

1. Pre-war neglect of the aircraft industry.
2. Indecision over the selection of the designs to be built.
3. Control by the automobile industry which was largely ignorant of aeronautics
4. Attempting to fit the Liberty engine to every design.

That the aircraft industry and the Signals Corps Aeronautical Division, which was its biggest potential customer, was largely neglected prior to America's entry into the war is a matter of fact and has already been described earlier in this book. With little established aeroplane manufacturing capacity, the aircraft manufacturing industry was forced to expand exponentially, with existing companies having to acquire greatly increased factory space in order to fulfil the sudden demand. However, all combatant nations faced similar demands and America's response was neither significantly worse, nor better, than that of her allies.

America entered the war at the beginning of April and, as already described, the Bolling Mission left for Europe some eight weeks later, and although Bolling's final report was not completed until mid-August, his recommendations were regularly updated, by cable, as it progressed. Any saving in time that may have been possible would not have materially influenced the programme's failure to reach, by mid-November 1918, the position it should have attained by the end of July. That some of the types selected for production subsequently proved unsuitable is more suggestive of decisions made in haste rather than any indecision. Nonetheless, orders were placed and then cancelled far too often, and a great deal of time, effort, and expense was wasted thereby. The Curtiss company, in particular, received several large orders for combat types, including the SPAD, the S.E.5, and the Bristol Fighter, only to have them cancelled, usually before any could be completed.

Congress, which included members of both parties, knowing little about either aeroplane manufacture or mass production methods, had been happy on entry into the war to place the programme in the hands of those who seemed jointly to know a great deal about both: the Joint Technical Board and the Aircraft Production Board. However, while the

Technical Board were experts in aeronautics, they knew little about actual manufacture and nobody involved realised the extent to which aeroplanes, as manufactured items, differ from motor cars. Cars, especially those of the period, are simple structures, robustly made, durable, and relatively heavy, whereas aeroplanes are complex, lightweight, relatively fragile, and made to strict tolerances. Their manufacture, by an industry not accustomed to such work, required a level of training, and of close inspection, this was not only not provided but simply not understood.

The Liberty engine made no advances in design or technology, being designed specifically for mass production in American factories, and had a similar power to weight ratio as that of other contemporary designs. It was therefore simply too heavy for installation in aeroplanes, such as the SPAD or Bristol Fighter, which had not been designed for engines of that power and thus of that weight. Only in the DH-4—which although not originally designed for that level of power, had already been developed to accommodate the dimensionally similar Rolls-Royce Eagle—did the V12 Liberty go to war in an American-built aeroplane. Fortunately, Liberty engine production, although delayed by development problems and never reaching the planned output rate, managed to keep pace with the equally reduced rate of aeroplane production.

However, while all these factors, which were obvious as early as the spring of 1918, contributed to the problems experienced in getting aeroplanes built and shipped to the front, the author believes that those responsible for planning of the whole programme were simply overconfident of America's ability to do things her own way. Instead of learning from the mistakes made by her allies, America chose to repeat them.

Mass production methods are best suited to simple components, of fixed and unchanging design, with fairly generous tolerances regarding fit and finish, not to the complex and constantly evolving nature of the combat aeroplanes of the time. No allowance was made for development nor for production problems, and similar contingencies that, although unpredictable, ought to have been expected. Such problems did arise and were largely overcome, and the rate of output was still accelerating when the war ended, suggesting that had the war continued, America might well have made good on its promise to 'darken the skies'.

The Republican Party made much political capital out of the shortcomings of the aircraft building programme, blaming their Democrat rivals, who had been in office for the last two terms, for America's lack of preparedness for war, for the vast expenditure and the obvious wastages, and for the consequent high taxation levels that followed, winning a landslide victory in the 1920 elections.

The 100th Aero Squadron poses with some of its DH-4s. Such photos were used to show the public how America was contributing to winning the war.

Another view of the assembled, but uncovered DH-4 at the Fisher Body factory.

Both Dayton-Wright and Fisher Body survived the alleged scandals and continued in aircraft manufacture until after the end of the war, fulfilling all un-cancelled orders. The Dayton-Wright Company was bought by General Motors in 1919 and attempted to manufacture aeroplanes of its own design, but it was closed down in 1923, with its design rights being acquired by the newly created Consolidated Aircraft Corporation based in Buffalo, New York.

GM also bought a majority stake in the Fisher Body company, returning it solely to the manufacture of motor car bodies, although the company again manufactured aircraft components during the Second World War.

After the end of the war, Edward Deeds went back to Delco, reacquiring his stock holding in the company and continuing to pursue his career in business.

APPENDIX I

# The Liberty Engine

Although designed to be produced in four-, six-, eight-, and twelve-cylinder versions, only the V12 type entered volume production and is here described. It was a direct drive engine with a bore of 5 inches, a stroke of 7 inches, and a dry weight of 820 lb. It was built in two versions: the Army type and the Navy type; the latter having a reduced compression ratio to reduce stress and increase reliability for long overwater flights when fitted to flying boats.

The Army type, which was by far the most numerous, had a compression ratio of 5.3:1 and developed a maximum of 425 hp at 1,750 rpm, with 405 hp at 1,650 rpm being its normal rating. The Navy version had a compression ratio of 4.78:1 and the maximum power output 396 hp.

## Cylinders

The design of the Liberty series of engines included individual cylinders, each formed from a steel tube, one end of which was closed to form the cylinder head and had the valve seats machined into it. The cylinders were fully interchangeable. The holding down flange was formed almost 3 inches from the open end, while the lower part of the cylinder was heated and was drilled for the studs that secured it to the crankcase. The water jacket was made in two pieces and welded in place, the joint being at right angles to the crank case. The water connections were also welded into place, as were the valve pockets and sparking plug bosses.

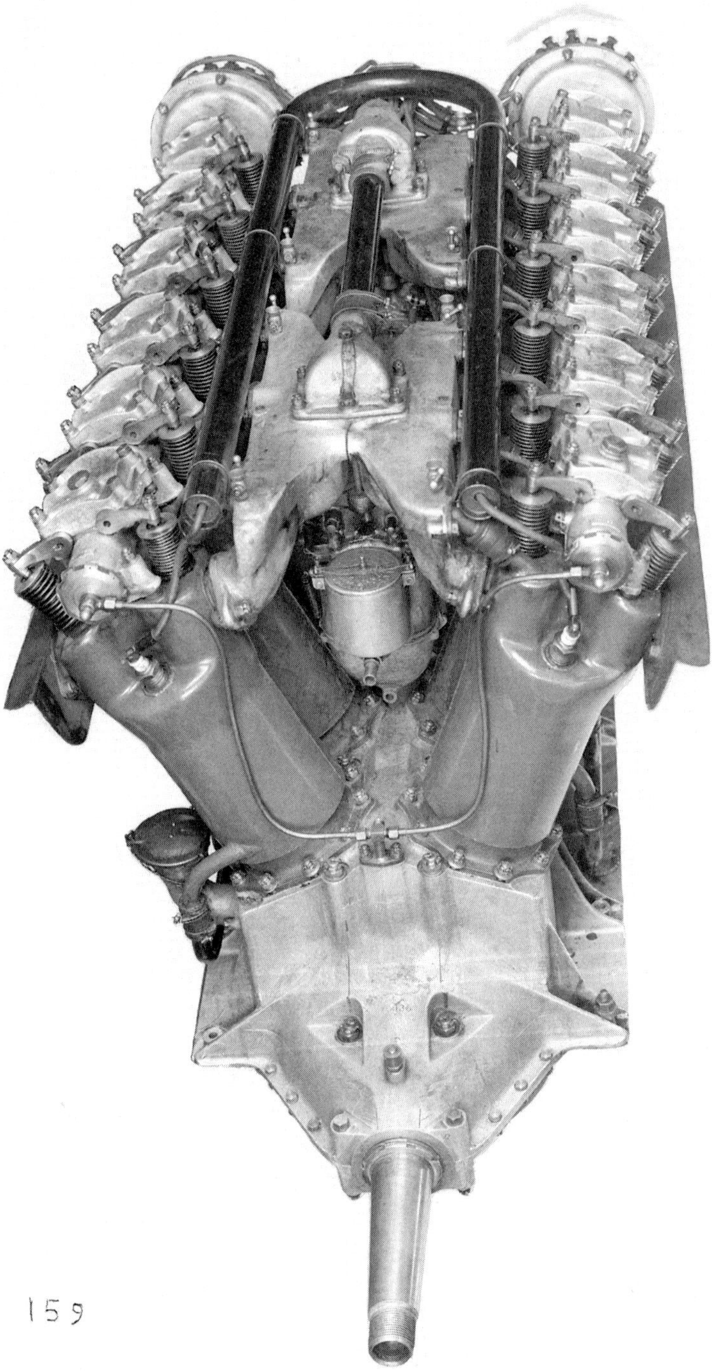

A three-quarter front view of the twelve-cylinder Liberty engine, showing the narrow angle between the cylinder banks.

## Pistons

The pistons were cast from aluminium alloy and had domed tops, flattened at the crown, with three compression rings fitted in grooves above the gudgeon pin. These rings each had a diagonal gap and a shallow oil groove machined into its face. Seven further oil groves were machined into the piston skirt. The gudgeon pins were of hollow steel tube and were allowed to float in the piston bushes, their outer ends being radiused to match the contour of the cylinder bore.

## Crankshaft

The forged steel crankshaft had six big end journals, one for each pair of cylinders, and was supported by seven phosphor bronze shell bearings, the one closest to the propeller being much longer than the remainder. A double thrust bearing was fitted between front main bearing and the tapered propeller hub.

## Connecting Rods

These were of the blade and fork type, with phosphor bronze little end bearings. Each blade rod was fitted with a phosphor bronze shell big end bearing, the forked rod having a white metal bearing running on the outside of the bearing shell of the blade rod. The forked end rods could be fitted to either bank of cylinders provided that all were fitted to the same side.

## Crankcase

The cast aluminium alloy crankcase was made in two halves joined horizontally (as is still common practice) in line with the centres of the main bearings. The upper portion attached to the lower by means of a bolted flange joint and was stiffened by seven pairs of cast ribs The lower part was generally flat bottomed, with an oil well at the front and rear ends. The rear of the crankcase housed the oil and water pumps and a connection for a hydraulic gun synchronisation gear was provided at the end of the crankshaft.

## Valve Gear

Each cylinder was fitted with two valves, inlet and exhaust, fitted in cast iron guides pressed into the valve pockets in the cylinder head and with their stems inclined at 13½ degrees to the cylinder axis. The exhaust valves were on the outside of each bank of cylinders, the inlets being on the inside, with the camshaft fitted in the included angle between them, operating the valves via machined steel rocker arms. The camshafts were driven by means of shafts and gear at half the rotational speed of the crankshaft, further connections to the gears also driving the pumps and the dynamo.

## Cooling System

A centrifugal water pump, driven at one and a half times the crankshaft speed, circulated the water (used as a coolant) via two long tapered manifolds, fitted one each side of the engine, below the level of the cylinder flanges.

Short branch pipes connected the manifold via rubber hoses to each cylinder water jacket, the outlet connections being on the induction manifold jackets from where the water was passed to the radiator and returned to the pump. A drain point was fitted below the water pump, as was a connection for a thermometer.

## Lubricating System

The pistons, gudgeon pins, and cylinder bores were lubricated by splash, oil being pumped to the remainder of the engine, including the camshafts and valve gear, the pumps being fitted below the oil well at the rear of the sump and comprising a double scavenge pump and a pressure pump. Internal arrangements of oil channels and pipes were designed to ensure that oil is returned to the pump even if the aeroplane was climbing or diving.

## Fuel System

Twin duplex carburettors were fitted beneath the junctions of the forward and rear induction manifolds and were fitted with manually operated mixture controls to compensate for the decreasing density of the atmosphere as the aeroplane reached greater altitudes. Petrol feed to the carburettors was normally by gravity.

## Ignition System

The ignition system was developed from the battery coil type commonly used on automobiles as the 45-degree angle between the cylinder banks. This precluded the use of a conventional twelve-cylinder magneto, which American industry was ill-equipped to manufacture anyway. Instead, a dynamo, driven from the same gear system as the pumps, maintained the charge in an 8-volt accumulator/battery from which current was supplied to two separate ignition systems, one for each set of sparking plugs, the very high current needed to create a spark being produced by means of a high tension coil. Twin 12 connection distributors were fitted at the rear of the engine and twin ignition switches mounted on the pilot's instrument board to isolate each system as required. Crews were warned that rapid operation of these switches, off and on, when the engine was warm or primed ready for starting could create a sufficient spark to inadvertently cause the engine to start.

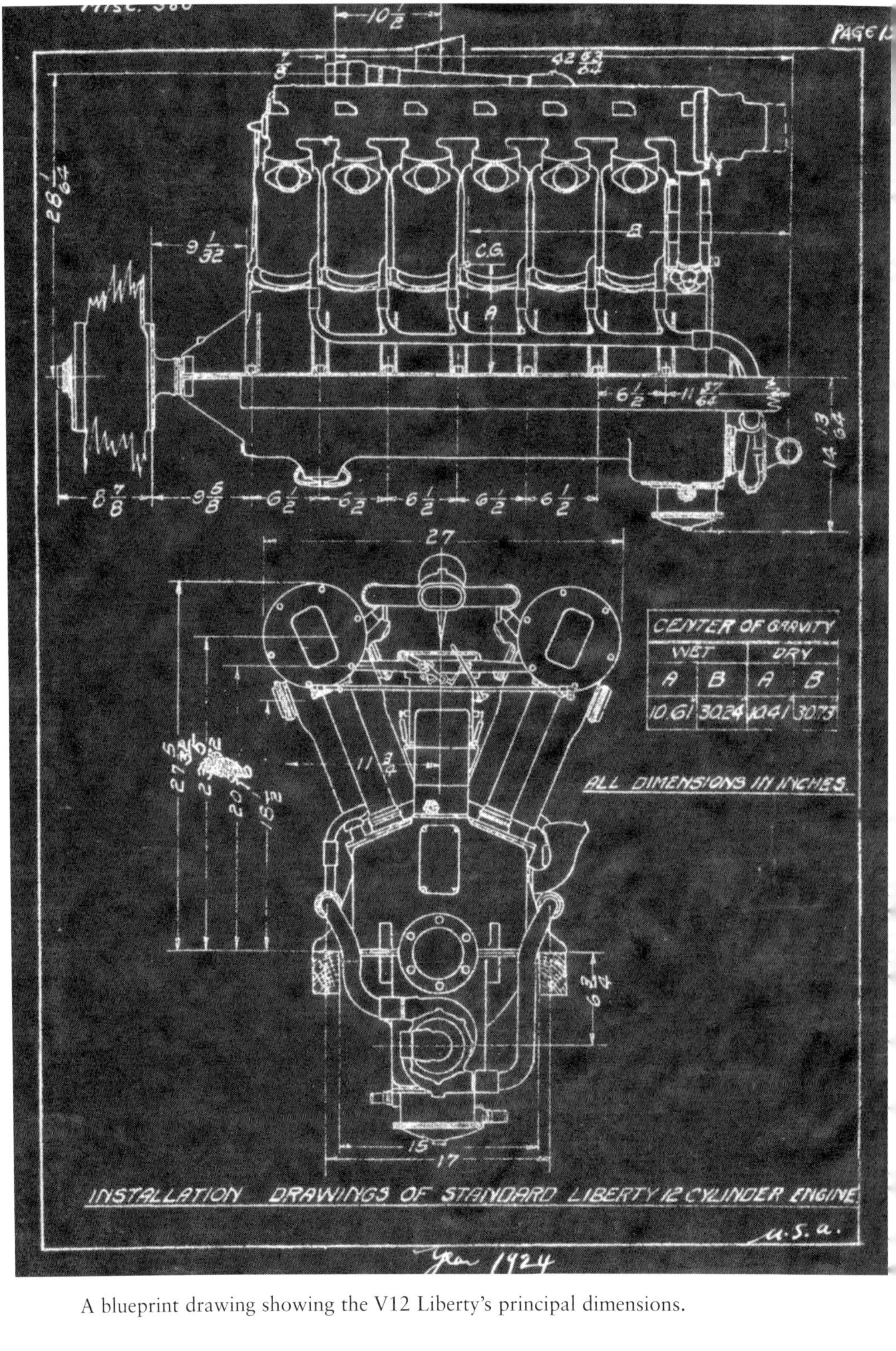


A blueprint drawing showing the V12 Liberty's principal dimensions.

# V12 Liberty Engine: Wartime Production

| | Packard | Lincoln | Ford | General Motor | Nordyke & Marmon |
|---|---|---|---|---|---|
| December 1917 | 21 | | | | |
| January 1918 | 40 | | | | |
| February 1918 | 70 | | | | |
| March 1918 | 107 | 15 | | | |
| April 1918 | 321 | 94 | | | |
| May 1918 | 452 | 127 | | | |
| June 1918 | 525 | 344 | 53 | 130 | |
| July 1918 | 681 | 484 | 182 | 225 | 16 |
| August 1918 | 650 | 751 | 519 | 325 | 42 |
| September 1918 | 627 | 687 | 812 | 177 | 59 |
| October 1918 | 903 | 1,050 | 1,059 | 558 | 308 |
| November 1918 | 636 | 818 | 1,201 | 424 | 143 |
| December 1918 | 572 | 1,109 | 124 | 151 | 241 |
| 1919 | 304 | 511 | | 537 | 191 |
| | | | | | |
| TOTAL | 5,960 | 5,990 | 3,950 | 1,827 | 990 |

At least 5,500 engines on order with Packard on wartime contracts were cancelled, as were 10,500 from Lincoln and the remainder of existing orders from Ford, General Motors, and Nordyke & Marmon. An order for 1,500 placed with the Duesenberg Company was also cancelled at the end of the war, without any engines being completed. The Trego Motor Corporation had been awarded an order for 500 engines, but after the first completed engine was delivered in August 1918 and examined, these were reassigned for use in tanks, a role for which the design was reintroduced in the Second World War.

Post-war developments of the Liberty design included versions that were variously air cooled, inverted, and supercharged, while war surplus examples found new homes in speedboats, racing cars, and in the 1925 world land speed record car 'Babs'.

APPENDIX II

# DH-4 Statistics

An exact total for DH-4 production up to the date of the Armistice has proved difficult to establish as the figures generally available are usual given month by month and because some aeroplanes, although delivered unassembled as spare parts, have been included in published totals for propaganda purposes. Even official sources vary, offering totals between 3,227 and 3,459, the latter figure appearing more likely when compared to the following table taken from US Government documents, which is generally considered to be as accurate as can be possible for overall production on wartime orders, including those completed after the Armistice.

| | Dayton-Wright | Fisher Body | Standard |
|---|---|---|---|
| February 1918 | 9 | | |
| March 1918 | 4 | | |
| April 1918 | 15 | | |
| May 1918 | 153 | | |
| June 1918 | 336 | | |
| July 1918 | 480 | | 4 |
| Aug 1918 | 124 | 96 | ? |
| Sept 1918 | 518 | 203 | ? |
| Oct 1918 | 556 | 502 | ? |
| Nov 1918 | 504 | 567 | ? |
| Dec 1918 | 200 | 227 | ? |
| 1919 | 202 | 2 | 1 |
| TOTAL | 3,101 | 1,600 | 140 |
| CANCELLED | 899 | 1,400 | 360 |

The total number of DH-4s shipped to France was 1,885, of which 667 reached the combat zone, although not all of those made it into action.

## DH-4s with in France on 11 November 1918

<table>
<tr><th>LOCATION</th><th>DEPOT</th><th>No. of DH-4s</th><th>TOTAL</th></tr>
<tr><td>The Front</td><td></td><td></td><td>196</td></tr>
<tr><td rowspan="3">Zone of Advance</td><td>First Depot</td><td>64</td><td rowspan="3">129</td></tr>
<tr><td>Fifth Depot</td><td>41</td></tr>
<tr><td>Advanced Depot</td><td>24</td></tr>
<tr><td rowspan="2">Service Supply Depots</td><td>Orly Depot</td><td>25</td><td rowspan="2">203</td></tr>
<tr><td>Remorantin Depot</td><td>178</td></tr>
<tr><td>Advanced Training</td><td></td><td>270</td><td>270</td></tr>
<tr><td>TOTAL</td><td></td><td></td><td>798</td></tr>
</table>

APPENDIX III

# Aircraft Production Facts

Between each nation's entry into the war and the Armistice of 11 November 1918, the total production figures, including training machines and, where applicable, machines assembled from salvaged spare parts, for the various combatant nations are as follows:

| Country | Aeroplanes | Engines |
|---|---|---|
| Great Britain | 55,003 | 41,034 |
| France | 67,982 | 83,317 |
| Germany | 47,637 | 40,449 |
| Italy | 20,000 (approx.) | 38,000 (approx.) |
| USA | 15,572 | 41,000 (approx.) |

As can be seen, Germany built more aeroplanes than she did engines, often making up the shortfall by salvaging engines from obsolete or crashed aeroplanes, including those of her enemies.

Britain relied heavily on France for engines throughout the war, and also bought engines from Italy and, towards the end of the war, from the US, including Curtiss OX-5s for training machines and Libertys, the latter, due to production delays, in fewer numbers than had been originally hoped.

# Bibliography

## Official Documents


Bolling, R. C., 'The Report of Aeronautical Commission', US National Archive, State Department paper 7112-56, 15 August 1917.

Cromwell, B., 'America's Munitions', US Government Printing Office, Washington DC, 1919.

Gorrell, E. S., 'The Early Activities of The Air Service', Washington DC, 1920.

Hughes, C. E., 'Report on Aircraft Production', Congressional Records, Washington DC, 1919.

Ministry of Munitions, 'The 12 Cylinder Liberty Engine Handbook'—London WC2, September 1918.

National Advisory Committee for Aeronautics, 'Annual Report', US Government Printing Office, Washington DC, 1917.

Senate Report No. 555, 'Aircraft Production in the United States', Washington DC, 22 August 1918.

The Office of Air Force History, 'The U.S. Air Service in WW1', Washington DC, 1978.

'The Signal Corps and Air Service: A Study of Their Expansion in the United States 1917–1918', War Department Document 1109, Washington DC, 1922.

'The War with Germany, a Statistical Summary', US Government Printing Office, Washington DC, 1919.

'The Yanks Were There—a Chronological and Documentary Review of WW1', US National Archive (undated).

'United States Army Aircraft production Facts', US Government Printing Office, Washington, DC, 1919.


## Books


Bowers, P. M., *The American D.H.4* (Letchworth: Profile Publications Ltd, 1966).

Bowyer, C., *Bristol F2b, King of Two Seaters* (London: Ian Allen, 1985); *Handley Page Bombers of the First World War* (Bourne End: Aston Publications, 1991).

Boyne, W. J., *The De Havilland DH-4* (Washington DC: Smithsonian Institute, 1961).
Bruce, J. M., *De Havilland Aircraft of WW1* (London: Arms & Armour Press, 1981).
Casari, R. B., *U.S. Army Aviation Serial Numbers* (Chillicothe, Ohio: Military Aircraft Publications, 1993).
Crouch, T., *The Bishop's Boys: A life of Wilbur and Orville Wright* (New York: Norton & Co., 1989).
Crowell, B., *The Road to France* (New Haven, Connecticut: Yale University Press, 1921).
Dickey, P. S., *The Liberty Engine 1919-1942* (Washington DC: Smithsonian Institute, 1968).
Gunston, B., *The Development of Piston Aero Engines* (London: Patrick Stevens Ltd, 2007).
Hatch, A., *Glenn Curtiss, Pioneer of Aviation* (Guildford, Connecticut: Lyon Press, 1940).
Howard, F., *Wilbur and Orville: A Biography of the Wright Brothers* (The University of Michigan, 1987).
Hudson, J. J., *Hostile Skies* (New York: Syracuse University Press, 1968).
Jane, F. T., *All the World's Aircraft—1919* (Newton Abbot, Devon: David & Charles, 1972).
Lamberton, W. M., *Fighter Aircraft of the 1914-18 War* (Letchworth: Harleyford, 1960); *Reconnaissance and Bomber Aircraft of the 1914-18 War* (Letchworth: Harleyford, 1962).
Lloyd, I., *Rolls Royce, The Growth of a Firm* (London: Macmillan, 1978).
Lyddon, W. G., *The War Missions to the United States 1914-1918* (Oxford: Oxford University Press, 1938).
MacFarland, M. W., (ed.), *The Papers of Wilbur and Orville Wright* (New York: McGraw Hill, 2000).
Maurer, M., (ed.), *The US Air Service in WW1* (Washington DC: Office of Air Force History, 1978).
Meulen, J., *The Politics of Aircraft; Building an American Military Industry* (University of Kansas, 1991).
Morrow, J. H., *The Great War in the Air* (Washington DC: Smithsonian Institute, 1993).
Penrose, H., *British Aviation; Great War and Armistice* (London: Putnam, 1969).
Prentice, A. M., *Pictorial Review of the Spruce Production Division* (Portland, Oregon: 1918).
Treadwell, F. C., *America's First Air War* (Shrewsbury: Airlife, 2000).
Setright, L. J. K., *The Power to Fly* (London: Allen & Unwin, 1972).
Shulman, S., *Unlocking the sky; Glenn Curtiss and the Race to Invent the Aeroplane* (New York: HarperCollins, 2002).
Strurtivent, R., and Page, G., *The S.E.5 File* (London: Air Britain, 1996).
Williams, W. A., *Against the Odds- The Life of Lionel Rees VC* (Clwyd, Wales: 1989).

## Periodicals

*Quarterly Journal, Cross and Cockade International* (England), various issues 1970 to 2013.

*Flight* (London, England), various issues 1910–1920.
*The New York Times* (New York, USA), various issues 1917–1918.
*Over The Front*, The League of World War 1 Aviation Historians (USA), various issues, 1995–2013.
*The Times* (London, England), various issues 1917–1919.
*WW1 Aero—The Journal of the early Aeroplane* (World War 1 Aeroplanes Inc., Poughkeepsie, USA), various issues 1972 to 2013.

# Index


AEF 49, 81, 86, 130, 132
Aircraft Board 37, 70, 96, 107, 119-120, 127
Aircraft Production Board 11, 26-27, 30, 37, 41-42, 44, 46, 51, 61, 64, 70, 72-73, 77, 80, 83-84, 87, 95, 105-106, 120, 140
Aircraft Manufacturing Co. 105, 111; DH-4 9, 36-38, 42, 47-48, 56, 64-65, 71, 75, 105-110; D.H.9 71, 106-110; D.H.9A 111
Alliance Aeroplane Co. 101
Aviation Act 60

Baker, Newton D. 22, 26, 30, 44, 47, 59, 108, 124
Balfour, Arthur 24-25
Barnwell, Frank 77, 89
Billing, Noel Pemberton 25
Bleriot, Louis 19
Board of Munitions 42
Bolling, Raynal C. 44-45, 47-49, 51, 58, 65, 70-72, 77, 84, 89, 95, 105, 107, 130, 140
Borglum, Gutzon 120-121
Breguet 51, 130
Brindley, Maj. O. 108
British & Colonial Aeroplane Co.; Bristol F.2B Fighter 47, 56, 58, 65, 71, 89-94, 114, 124, 140-141; Bristol Scout 47, 56, 58, 77-79
British Government 14, 52-53, 67, 81, 98
Buick Motor Company 36, 62, 66, 133
Bureau of Aircraft Production 70, 120
Bureau of Standards 34-35, 69
Burnside, Frank 78

Caproni, Gianni 49, 95
Caproni Company 49, 96-97; biplane 57, 96-97; triplane 50, 57, 71, 96-98
Cadillac Car Company 33, 35, 62, 66
Chanute, Octave 15
Childs, Lt W. G. 44, 49
Clark, Capt. V. E. 44, 49, 57, 89, 92, 96, 98
Cody, S. F. 14
Coffin, Howard E. 11, 27, 30, 32, 42, 46
Congress 21-23, 26, 30, 60, 64, 124, 138, 140
Consolidated Aircraft Corp. 144
Cowdray, Lord 47
Curtiss, Glenn 13, 15-16
Curtiss Aeroplane & Motor Co. 20, 22, 27, 39 , 41, 62, 74, 81, 84, 91-92, 97, 110, 113, 133, 140; Curtiss JN-4 37-38, 69, 72-73, 75, 77, 120; Curtiss OX-5 engine 37, 73, 75, 154; Curtiss R-4 40, 87-88; Curtiss V-2-3 engine 87
Council of National Defence 22, 26-27, 70, 120

D.H.4 *See Aircraft Manufacturing Co.*
DH-4 107-113, 117, 122-124, 130, 132, 134, 138-139, 141, 144, 152-153
D.H.9 *See Aircraft Manufacturing Co.*
Damm, Lt-Col. H. 108

Day, Charles H. 75
Dayton, Ohio 24, 28, 62, 64, 78, 81, 91, 94, 105, 109, 114, 120, 123-124
Dayton Wright Airplane Co. 41, 62, 63, 71, 73, 94, 106-107, 110, 113, 122, 140, 144, 152
Deeds, Edward A. 27-28, 31-32, 61, 64, 120, 122, 124-125, 144
De Havilland, Geoffrey 9, 105, 111
Delco 28, 34, 62, 144
Dept. of Military Aeronautics 70
Disque, Brig-Gen. D. P. 67
Doolittle, Lt J. 91-92
Durant, William C. 66
Dusenberg Motor Corporation 118

Eberhart Steel Products Co. 83

Farman, Henri 13
Fisher Body Co. 39, 41, 62, 63, 69-70, 73, 75, 77, 96-97, 106, 113, 117, 122-123, 140, 144
*Flight* magazine 61
Folland, Henry 80
Fort Myer 17-18
Fort Sam Houston 18, 21
Ford, Henry 11, 23
Ford Motor Company 62, 65-66, 151
Foulois, Benjamin D. 18, 26, 55, 59, 100, 108, 128
Franklin, Mr P. 127
French Government 11, 22, 29-30, 39, 51, 53-54

General Motors 66, 144, 151
General Vehicle Company 22, 40
Gifford, Walter S. 120
Glendinning, Maj. R. 44-45, 51
Glenn L. Martin Co. 20, 103
Goodden, Frank 80
Gorrell, Edgar 26, 44
Grand Rapids Airplane Co. 101

Hailman, Mr C. H. 44
Hall, Elbert J. 32, 66
Hall, Maj. J. E. 91
Hall-Scott Motor Company 22, 32-33, 66; A7 engine 37, 73, 75
Handley Page O/400 71, 98-99, 101-103
Hispano-Suiza 22, 31, 39-40, 51-53, 56-58, 71, 74, 80-81, 83-86, 90, 92
House of Representatives 59-60
Hudson Car Company 27, 32
Hughes, Charles E. 120, 122, 125
Hughes, Herbert 44, 49, 51
Humphreys, Lt F. E. 18
Hunt, Mr O. E. 35
Hurley, Mr W. B. 44

Industrial Preparedness Committee 27
Isotta Franschini 57, 95, 97

Joffre, Gen. 127
Joint Army & Navy Technical Board 26, 29-30, 35, 37, 41, 80, 140

Field, Kelly 81
Kettering. Charles F. 28
King, Col. C. B. 118
Kilner, Maj. 36
Kohn, Gen. 30

LUSAC 114-116, 118
L. W. F. 22
LaGuardia, F. H. 120
Lahm, Lt F. P. 18
Langley field 95
Liberty Bonds 60
Liberty engine 12, 33-34, 36, 61, 65-66, 85, 87, 89, 91-92, 94, 96, 101, 106-108, 111, 114, 119, 124-125, 132, 138, 140-141, 145-151
Lorraine Detreich 33, 40

McCook Field 64, 78-79, 81, 92, 94, 105, 107, 111-114
Macready, Lt J. A. 117
Marlin machine gun 91, 94, 114
Marmier, Lt de 114-115
Marmon, Mr H. C. 44, 47, 49, 56
Martin, Glenn L. 20, 62, 103
Martinsyde F3 71
Mercedes 33
Mitchell, William 35, 42, 49
Montgomery, Robert L. 27, 28, 61
Mowry, Mr R. I. 45
Mullins Steel Boat Co. 101

NACA 20
National Cash Register Company 27
*New York Herald* 120
Nieuport 49, 51, 78, 130, 135
Nordyke & Marmon 44, 66, 151

Oler, Lt W. M. 92

Packard Car Company 28, 31-32, 34-36, 44-45, 65--66, 114-115, 117, 151
Pere, Georges le 111, 115
Perfetti, Maj. R. 26, 96
Pershing, Gen. J. 47, 59, 65, 71, 85, 105, 107-108, 130
Pierce-Arrow 39

Ryan, John D. 70, 120
Rees VC, L. W. B. 24-25
Le Rhône engine 22, 53, 56-57, 77-78
Ribot, Alexandre 29, 42, 119
Rolls-Royce 5, 33, 56-57, 65; Eagle 38-39, 105-106, 141; Falcon 58, 89, 91
Roosevelt, Theodore 15
Rothermere, Lord 100
Royal Aircraft Factory 39, 80; S.E.5 39, 48, 80, 84
Royal Flying Corps (RFC) 19-20, 24, 29, 38, 47, 73, 77, 80, 89, 98, 128
Royal Naval Air Service (RNAS) 73, 77, 87, 98

S.E.5 *see Royal Aircraft Factory*
SPAD 49, 51, 53, 65, 71, 77, 80-81, 84-86, 124, 130, 134, 140-141
Santos-Dumont, Alberto 13
Schroeder, Capt. R. W. 117
Selfridge, Lt T. 18
Selfridge Field 81
Sheppard, Senator Morris 120
Shipping Control Committee 127
Signal Corps 15, 17-22, 34, 44, 59, 67, 70, 73, 75, 91, 111, 128; Aeronautical Section 42, 44, 128; Aviation Section 19-21, 24, 59, 60, 127; Construction Division 61; Engineering Division 61; Spruce Production Division 67-68
Sopwith Aeroplane Co. 40, 71, 73, 78; Sopwith Camel 42, 47, 70
Squier, George O. 18, 24, 27, 51, 59, 122
Standard Aircraft Corp. 69, 75, 96, 101; J-1 73, 75-76, 124

Taylor, Admiral David W. 27
Trego Motor Corporation. 66, 151
Thomas, Benjamin D. 73, 78
Thomas Morse Airplane Company 21, 40, 77-79, 110

Vail, Mr R. A. 44, 49
Vincent, Jesse G. 31-32, 61

Waldon, Sidney D. 27-28, 61, 128
War Department 26
Washington DC 24, 31, 35, 43, 51, 55, 64, 77, 80, 105
Weir, Sir William 31
Westervelt, Cdr G. C. 44, 48
Westland Aircraft Co. 111
Willards Hotel 32
Wilbur Wright Field 81, 91, 114
Wilson, Woodrow 23, 29, 60, 120
Wittemann-Lewis 122
Wright Brothers 13, 15-16, 22; Wright, Orville 17-18, 20, 122; Wright, Wilbur 16, 18, 20, 120
Wright Company 20, 62, 64, 103, 122
Wright *Flyer* 14-15, 17-19
Wright-Martin 20, 22, 27, 39, 62, 75, 81, 103

USD-9 111-113, 117
US Government 11, 14, 20, 26, 47, 97, 120, 152
US Senate 23, 60, 122, 123
Union Switch & Signal Co. 78

Zenith carburettor 33